Concepts of Chivalry in
Sir Gawain and the Green Knight

CONCEPTS OF CHIVALRY

in

Sir Gawain and the Green Knight

By
Wendy Clein

PILGRIM BOOKS
NORMAN, OKLAHOMA

Published by Pilgrim Books
P.O. Box 2399, Norman, Oklahoma 73070
Copyright © 1987 by Pilgrim Books
Manufactured in the U.S.A. First edition. All rights reserved.

Library of Congress Cataloging-in-Publication Data

Clein, Wendy.
  Concepts of chivalry in Sir Gawain and
the Green Knight.

  Bibliography: p.
  Includes index.
  1. Gawain and the Grene Knight.   2. Gawain
(Legendary character)—Romances—History and
criticism.   3. Chivalry in literature.
4. Death in literature.   5. Reader-response
criticism.   I. Title.
PR2065.G31C47   1987   821'.1   86-30653
ISBN: 0-937664-75-8

For Elizabeth Salter

Contents

Illustrations

Preface

hen I began this study, I thought that an investigation
of fourteenth-century chivalry would resolve conflicts
in scholarly discussions of *Sir Gawain and the Green
Knight*. According to my original hypothesis, contradictory evaluations of the poem resulted from modern readers'
incomplete understanding of medieval attitudes toward chivalry.
I hoped that my study would resolve questions about the seriousness of the hero's fault and the poem's judgment of secular
chivalry. Instead I found that chivalric texts themselves embodied
numerous oppositions. Celebrated by heralds as a cultural ideal
and upheld by moralists as an example of vice, knighthood
appears in a range of conflicting guises. *Sir Gawain and the
Green Knight* investigates the paradoxes of fourteenth-century
chivalry.

The introductory chapter explores the way in which the narrative structure of *Sir Gawain and the Green Knight* elicits
questions. The poem fails to resolve a number of issues, in
particular the validity of Gawain's pentangle chivalry and the
meaning of his response to death. The first part of the book
examines these issues as they are expressed in wills, sermons, and
treatises, to illustrate the oppositions existing within medieval
approaches to knighthood and mortality. Part Two analyses *Sir*

Gawain and the Green Knight in the light of this cultural context, showing how the poem's competing perspectives invite rather than answer questions.

Rather than eliminating possibilities for interpretation, my study draws attention to the open-endedness of *Sir Gawain and the Green Knight*. This conception of the poem's ending challenges accepted notions of medieval art, adhering more closely to contemporary theories of reading that value textual indeterminacy. Part Three turns to other fourteenth-century works where, I argue, textual open-endedness also characterizes the poetry.

In the process of completing this work I have benefited from much advice and encouragement. My interest in the subject began when I was a student in Elizabeth Salter's seminar on Medieval Literature and Society at the University of Connecticut. She encouraged my investigation and agreed to act as my dissertation director. Her death was a great personal loss and a loss to all medievalists. I am grateful for all she taught me in the year I knew her. As I have struggled with the contradictions of chivalric texts, I have often thought of the delight she took in the complexities of history and literature. This work has always, in a sense, been dedicated to her.

I have been fortunate in having the help of other fine scholars during the course of this work. Charles Owen directed my dissertation after Elizabeth's death, and I profited from his extensive understanding of the Middle Ages. Derek Pearsall gave very generously of his time and knowledge and offered much helpful criticism. Margaret Higonnet helped me become more conscious of the theoretical assumptions of scholarly discourse and offered astute criticism. I thank David Benson for valuable advice and for many delightful conversations about medieval literature. I am indebted to Bennett Brockman and Thomas Jambeck for introducing me to medieval studies as well as for their advice in the course of this study. Without the assistance of these fine scholars and of many other friends and colleagues who have given encouragement and advice, this book would be a much poorer thing; I cannot thank them enough.

I am indebted to Chris Ray, my student assistant at Rhodes College, for his help with the index. I am also grateful for the assistance of the Interlibrary Loan Department at the University of Connecticut, of Princeton University's Index of Christian Art, of the Bodleian Library and the British Library. I thank the British Library for permission to reproduce photographs from their collection and the Rector of Dorchester Abbey for permission to reproduce a photograph of the Dorchester knight, taken by my husband, Bob. I acknowledge the generous support of the University of Connecticut's Research Foundation. Finally, to Bob and Phoebe, thank you for the love that sustains me.

PART ONE

The Medieval Conflictus

Chapter 1

Sir Gawain and the Green Knight and Its Readers

nly when we finish reading a work can we evaluate its meaning as a whole, the way in which its parts fit together. At the conclusion of a tale, the quest to discover what happens next ceases. We discover whether our predictions are accurate, whether the work meets or violates our expectations. *Sir Gawain and the Green Knight* concludes in a way that thwarts our desire for resolution. The poem withholds motives and explanations until the end. Then, contrary to readers' expectations, the problems that *Sir Gawain and the Green Knight* entertains are not resolved upon the completion of the hero's quest and the antagonist's revelation of his identity and purpose. Like Gawain, readers are surprised by the disclosure of the Green Knight's identity with Bertilak and his wife's complicity in the test. Moreover, the news that Gawain's aunt, Morgan la Faye, instigates the entire plot comes as a puzzling revelation. The discoveries at the end of the poem frustrate readers' satisfaction in Gawain's escape from harm, unleashing a host of questions. Rather than resolving uncertainties, the poem's conclusion forces readers to review the action and attempt to interpret it.

The indeterminate ending of *Sir Gawain and the Green Knight* ensures the reader's engagement in the problem of judgment. Although the poem is neatly framed by the self-referring context of "þe Brutus bokez" (line 2523),[1] the sense of closure is artificial, for the poem raises moral questions without finally resolving them. When the hero's quest is over, various characters in the poem offer different interpretations of the action. Because Gawain loved his life, Bertilak forgives him for concealing the girdle and judges him to be "as perle bi þe quite pese" (line 2364). Arthur and the court rejoice that Gawain returns unscathed, "al in sounde" (line 2489), and they adopt the green baldric to do him honor. For the hero, by contrast, the girdle has become "þe token of vntrawþe" (line 2509), and he judges himself permanently marred by his slip. By offering these varied and partial perspectives on the hero's quest and by withholding any authorial resolution of the resulting contradictions, *Sir Gawain and the Green Knight* draws readers into the pursuit of meaning.

The poem addresses first-time readers, creating suspense through structure and narratorial comment. For example, the narrator builds readers' apprehension by presenting the journey to the green chapel largely from Gawain's center of consciousness. Tension mounts as the guide sketches a fearful portrait of the Green Knight.[2] Gawain's anxiety grows as he inspects the desolate site of his encounter, "Debatande with hymself quat hit be myȝt" (line 2179). The hero's troubled imagination transforms the desolate landscape into a diabolical scene: "'Here myȝt aboute mydnyȝt / Þe dele his matynnes telle!'" (lines 2187–88).

The Green Knight slowly reveals himself, first through the noise of his ax, then through his command that Gawain abide, and finally in his approach, as he whirls out from behind the rocks, vaults a stream with the aid of his huge ax, and advances toward the hero. The interchange between the two and the feigned strokes of the ax draw out the suspense so that readers share Gawain's sense of relief as he escapes his obligation with only a nick and springs into action to take up the offensive.

1. *Sir Gawain and the Green Knight*, ed. J. R. R. Tolkien and E. V. Gordon, 2d ed., rev. Norman Davis. All quotations from the poem are from this edition.
2. A. C. Spearing, *The Gawain Poet*, p. 187.

Gawain's release is as powerful as a rebirth: "Neuer syn þat he watz burne borne of his moder / Watz he neuer in þis worlde wyȝe half so blyþe" (lines 2321–22). The elation which first-time readers perhaps share with the hero is only temporary, however. The revelation of the Green Knight's identity and the connection between the two games demands that Gawain's behavior be examined minutely and judged.

Subsequent readings of *Sir Gawain and the Green Knight* offer experiences that are different from and more aesthetically gratifying than the first. Of course, the poem eternally invites familiar readers to reenact the pleasurable experience of suspense. Once the resolution is known, the poem offers the more aesthetic experience of observing the narrator's technique in manipulating expectations. Our responses to characters alter too. Readers can appreciate Bertilak's skill in winning Gawain's confidence and the lady's artistry and wit in beguiling him. Correspondences that a first reader might not notice become apparent, such as the green-and-gold decoration of both the Green Knight and the lady's girdle.[3] Subtle ironies also become more noticeable, for example, Gawain's choice of a blue mantle (the color symbolizing loyalty) on the evening he breaks his pact to exchange winnings.[4] Finally, the questions the poem poses about chivalric ideals and human experience remain open for readers' consideration.

J. A. Burrow proposes that the narrative art of *Sir Gawain and the Green Knight* owes much to the nature of oral recitation and that the Gawain poet "made a virtue of necessity and positively exploited the linear character of the medium," most obviously by keeping readers in suspense.[5] Nevertheless, Burrow's own comparison of *Sir Gawain and the Green Knight* and *Beowulf* illustrates that the oral tradition offered a wide range of narrative possibilities and that the Gawain poet was not in any way bound by necessity.[6] As Burrow subsequently admits, the suspense of *Sir*

3. J. A. Burrow, *A Reading of* Sir Gawain and the Green Knight, p. 103.
4. Ibid., p. 112.
5. Ibid., p. 2.
6. Ibid., pp. 2–3. *Beowulf* excludes suspense through the use of narrative flashback and flash-forward. It is both thematic and encyclopedic.

Gawain and the Green Knight is more than the happy adaptation of literary circumstances. He argues that it enables the poet to "allow his 'meaning,' like his 'plot,' to emerge gradually from among a number of more or less deliberately countenanced possibilities."[7] If it were true that the poet intends a particular meaning to emerge, there would surely be more critical consensus. Instead, the linear narrative pattern gives readers the freedom to suspend judgment until the completion of the narrative, whereupon the open-ended conclusion elicits a consideration of the competing evaluations of knightly behavior evoked in the various interpretations of Gawain's lapse.

While the poem offers divergent evaluations of the hero's behavior in the responses of Gawain, Bertilak, and Arthur's court, critics tend to favor a particular interpretation, denying the validity of its opposite. Readers emphasizing the poem's comic aspects view the tolerant laughter of Bertilak and Arthur's court as sanative and Gawain's remorse as morbidly excessive.[8] Other readers, focusing on the poem's serious elements, condemn the laughter as trivializing or corrosive, a sign of ignorance rather than sanity.[9]

A less common response to the poem's ending is to offer a

7. Ibid., p. 3.

8. Arthur T. Broes, "*Sir Gawain and the Green Knight*: Romance as Comedy," *Xavier University Studies* 4 (1965): 35–54. Other readers opposed to Gawain's point of view include Larry Benson, *Art and Tradition in Sir Gawain and the Green Knight*; R. H. Bowers, "Gawain and the Green Knight as Entertainment," *MLQ* 24 (1963): 333–41; Dorothy Everett, *Essays on Middle English Literature*, p. 79; Richard Hamilton Green, "Gawain's Shield and the Quest for Perfection," *ELH* 29 (1962): 121–39; Donald R. Howard, *The Three Temptations: Medieval Man in Search of the World*, p. 248; Tony Hunt, "Gawain's Fault and the Moral Perspectives of *Sir Gawain and the Green Knight*," *Trivium* 10 (1975): 1–18; Richard M. Trask, " Sir Gawain's Unhappy Fault," *SSF* 16 (1979): 1–9.

9. Peter Christmas, "A Reading of Sir Gawain and the Green Knight," *Neophil* 58 (1974): 238–47. Other interpretations favoring Gawain's response include R. A. Halpern, "The Last Temptation of Gawain: Hony Soit Qui Mal Pence," *ABR* 23 (1972): 353–84; Nicolas Jacobs, "Gawain's False Confession," *ES* 51 (1970): p. 434; Robert C. Pierle, "*Sir Gawain and the Green Knight*: A Study in Moral Complexity," *SoQ* (1968), 203–11; Gordon M. Shedd, "Knight in Tarnished Armour: The Meaning of *Sir Gawain and the Green Knight*," *MLR* 62 (1967): 3–13; Lynn Staley Johnson, *The Voice of the Gawain-Poet*, pp. 89–91.

reading that recognizes the validity of more than one perspective. While A. C. Spearing leans toward a reading wherein Gawain appears slightly comic in his self-criticism, he accepts the validity of an opposing interpretation and concludes that *Sir Gawain and the Green Knight* is a poem "more 'open-ended' than the poet's three others, because it is not firmly placed in a perspective of absolute values."[10] Victor Yelverton Haines discusses the poem's contrasting perspectives in his study of the *felix culpa* doctrine in *Sir Gawain and the Green Knight*. He argues that both repentance and joy are proper responses to Gawain's failing; nevertheless, he concludes that Gawain's response is less complete than the court's, for at the poem's end the hero has not come to appreciate the operation of divine grace.[11] While also favoring the court's joyous response, Larry Benson sympathizes with Gawain's point of view, attributing the poem's balance to a "characteristically Gothic acceptance of life both as it is and as it should be."[12] J. A. Burrow describes the poem's final scene as an "ambiguous tableau," but he finds more agreement between conflicting viewpoints than the text truly affords: "The knights and ladies share the baldric with Gawain as a sign both of their corporate renown and their common humanity."[13] Although attempts to harmonize competing viewpoints are appealing, the poem offers no real evidence to suggest that other characters understand Gawain's point of view. On the hero's return, we hear none of the dialogue between Gawain and the court. The laughter at the end of the poem has the effect of distancing the hero from other Round Table knights. Although attempts to reconcile the disparate points of view address the poem's diversity, they impose limits on its open-ended structure by offering a resolution to a problem which is deliberately left unsolved.

The history of scholarship on *Sir Gawain and the Green Knight* demonstrates both the diversity of readers and the open

10. Spearing, *The* Gawain *Poet*, p. 235.
11. Victor Yelverton Haines, *The Fortunate Fall of Sir Gawain*, pp. 119–21.
12. Benson, *Art and Tradition*, p. 248.
13. Burrow, *A Reading of* Sir Gawain, p. 159.

nature of the text. No particular response to Gawain's adventures emerges as the most valid. Instead, the final indeterminacy of the poem makes it continually available for new interpretations, keeping it vital despite the passage of centuries.[14] Rather than attempting to close its open structure, substituting narrow interpretations for its polysemy, readers should concentrate on further exploring the problems it poses.

In arguing that the structure of *Sir Gawain and the Green Knight* frustrates the reader's search for a single meaning, I am rejecting the widely held theory that any tensions readers find in medieval art result from the distorting lens of their modern perspective. D. W. Robertson and his followers claim that only by using exegetical methods to interpret medieval texts can readers restore a sense of historicity.[15] In Robertson's view, medieval people perceived their world as hierarchical, without polarities or unresolved questions.[16] While this approach illuminates some medieval works of art, especially those of a propagandistic nature, it represents the Middle Ages as more uniform, more orthodox than is warranted. Although some romances promote traditional concepts of reality,[17] *Sir Gawain and the Green Knight* forces readers to evaluate fourteenth-century conventions and ideologies. The established idea of medieval readers and their culture needs to be reevaluated, for *Sir Gawain and the Green Knight* reflects tensions between chivalry and Christianity that were part of fourteenth-century experience.

Recent theories of reader reception offer a more flexible approach to *Sir Gawain and the Green Knight* than do exegetical methods. As much as other elements of a text, readers need to be

14. See Hans Robert Jauss's discussion of open, indeterminate structures in *Toward an Aesthetic of Reception*, trans. Timothy Bahti, p. 69.

15. D. W. Robertson's approach is set out in *A Preface to Chaucer*.

16. Ibid., pp. 3–51.

17. The genre of courtly romance has been represented as universally celebrating the values of the prevailing system; see Wolfgang Iser, *The Act of Reading*; and Erich Auerbach, *Mimesis: The Representation of Reality in Western Literature*, trans. W. A. Trask. *Sir Gawain and the Green Knight* is frequently interpreted as a statement of traditional morality.

taken into account, for they are integral to the discovery of meaning. Although Robertson claims authenticity for his approach by portraying the medieval reader as an exegete, this narrowly defined role prompts modern interpreters to censor many legitimate readings of medieval texts. While some texts cast readers as exegetes and reward a Robertsonian approach, many, including *Sir Gawain and the Green Knight*, do not.

An alternative approach is to attempt to identify the actual fourteenth-century readers of *Sir Gawain and the Green Knight*. Nonetheless, speculations about the poem's original audience, though interesting, are likely to remain inconclusive. A. C. Spearing argues that aristocratic details in the poem suggest that courtly life was "known and felt from the inside."[18] Elizabeth Salter and Michael Bennett have produced fascinating studies of the cultural milieu of northwestern aristocratic households, showing how it would support a production like *Sir Gawain and the Green Knight*.[19] Nevertheless, Derek Pearsall points out several problems inherent in attempts to identify the poem's original readers: "The audience implied may not be the audience addressed; the circumstances of manuscript survival may be no guide at all to the circumstances of production; and sophistication is a difficult thing to quantify."[20]

Fortunately, identifying a specific historical audience is not essential in interpreting *Sir Gawain and the Green Knight*, for the poem creates its readers, fictionalizing them in the text.[21] This "inscribed" role affects interpretation as much as do other

18. Spearing, *The* Gawain *Poet*, p. 8.

19. Elizabeth Salter, "The Alliterative Revival," *MP* 64 (1966): 146–50, 233–37; Michael J. Bennett, *Community, Class and Careerism: Cheshire and Lancashire Society in the Age of Sir Gawain and the Green Knight.*

20. Derek Pearsall, "The Alliterative Revival: Origins and Social Backgrounds," in David Lawton, ed., *Middle English Alliterative Poetry and Its Literary Background*, p. 49.

21. For discussions of the way in which writers construct roles for their audiences, see Walter J. Ong, "The Writer's Audience Is Always a Fiction," *PMLA* 90 (January, 1975): 9–21; and Iser, *The Act of Reading*, chap. 2.

elements, such as character or plot.[22] Nevertheless, the reader's role in *Sir Gawain and the Green Knight* is not uniform. The poem invites readers to adopt a variety of attitudes. Rather than viewing the poem from a single vantage point such as Christian moralism, critics must take into account the shifting perspectives from which the poem allows readers to interpret the action.

Sir Gawain and the Green Knight follows the tradition of oral poetry and addresses readers as if they are physically present, asking them to "lysten" (line 30) and "be stylle" (line 1996). These injunctions should not be taken to imply that the poem was composed orally, or even necessarily that it was designed to be read aloud, though this is possible.[23] Instead they indicate that readers are to cast themselves as the audience at the recitation of an Arthurian romance. The fictitious readers, the "ȝe" whom the narrator addresses directly, could include all the members of an aristocratic household: lords, ladies, clerks, and retainers. While actual readers may have been lay or clerical, noble or common, the poem speaks as if their world is not far removed from its courtly milieu. The descriptions of hunting, feasts, and architecture would confirm the values of those who belonged to the aristocracy. At the same time, such details would educate the nonaristocrat.

Since medieval courtly values are inscribed in the poem, modern readers are transported back in history and initiated into that milieu.[24] Consider, for example, the description of the New Year's feast at Camelot. The poem gently instructs readers in courtly etiquette while at the same time flattering us with the fiction that we are insiders: "Alle þis mirþe þay maden to þe mete tyme; / When þay had waschen worþyly þay wenten to sete, / Þe best burne ay abof, as hit best semed" (lines 71–73). Readers do

---

22. Iser, *The Act of Reading*, p. 33.

23. Richard Green presents evidence that, along with such things as gambling, caroling, dancing, chess, and cockfighting, public readings were regular courtly entertainment. Richard Firth Green, *Poets and Princepleasers*, pp. 54–59.

24. Iser notes that modern readers can reconstruct social norms from a text. Iser, *The Act of Reading*, p. 74.

not need to be familiar with courtly ritual and precedent to appreciate the decorum of Camelot, for the text demands our approval with the adverb *worþyly* and the parenthetical remark on seemliness.

During much of the poem fictional readers accept the values of courtly life. Nevertheless, at certain junctures, the poem appeals to the reader in a different character. A striking example of the deliberate rupture of the fictitious reader's consistency occurs at the start of the second fitt. During most of the first fitt the narrator's description of the action calls for our approval. Abruptly the tone changes, as the narrator condemns the hero (lines 495–99):

> Gawain watz glad to begin þose gomnez in halle,
> Bot þaȝ þe ende be heuy haf ȝe no wonder;
> For þaȝ men ben mery in mynde quen þay han mayn drynk,
> A ȝere ȝernes ful ȝerne, and ȝeldez neuer lyke,
> Þe forme to þe fynisment foldez ful selden.

The first fitt presents "gomnez" favorably as appropriate to courtly festivities. The mirth of Camelot's New Year is part of the decorum of its rituals. But the subsequent criticism of "mayn drynk" wrenches readers out of the courtly mode and demands that we become moralists, viewing the elapsed narrative in another context. Although the tendency in medieval criticism is to assign more validity to the moralist perspective than to the alternate aristocratic point of view, approaching *Sir Gawain and the Green Knight* in this way denies its inherent ambiguity. The narrator's comment here undermines the authority of the didactic mode, for nothing in Gawain's impeccable behavior of the first fitt suggests inebriation. Nevertheless, the moralist censure dislodges readers from the comfortable position of unquestioningly accepting the courtly point of view.

The conflicting roles assigned readers of *Sir Gawain and the Green Knight* bring into focus competing ethical systems in fourteenth-century culture. While the poem educates us in courtly and moralist values, these major medieval modes of ordering reality can be considerably sharpened through the study of the poem's cultural context. The attempt to regain a sense of the poem's dynamic relationship to the time of its composition is not mere antiquarianism. At its initial reception the major issues of *Sir Gawain and the Green Knight* held an immediacy which time has diminished. The poem rewards efforts to recover the extratextual setting with a richer sense of its implications. The competing perspectives in the poem are reflected in fourteenth-century approaches to chivalry and death, two major themes which studies of the poem have not yet explored in any depth.

The passage of time has obscured the meaning and importance of chivalry, a central value of the poem. In 1961, in an essay evaluating the state of criticism on *Sir Gawain and the Green Knight*, Morton Bloomfield suggested that the poem should be connected to the wider issues of the fourteenth century, among which he identified chivalry.[25] To date no study has addressed the complex phenomenon of knighthood found in *Sir Gawain and the Green Knight*. With the exception of two essays by historians,[26] discussions of chivalry in the poem have accepted Huizinga's theory of chivalric decadence in the fourteenth century.[27] To view chivalry as degenerate oversimplifies the complex picture that fourteenth-century culture offers. A familiarity with the literature of chivalry illuminates the poem by clarifying the cultural origins of its range of perspective.

25. Morton W. Bloomfield, "*Sir Gawain and the Green Knight*: An Appraisal," *PMLA* 76 (1961): 7–19.

26. Maurice Keen, "Chivalrous Culture in Fourteenth Century England," *Historical Studies* 10 (1976): 1–24; and Gervase Mathew, "Ideals of Knighthood in Late Fourteenth Century England," in *Studies in Medieval History Presented to F. M. Powicke*, pp. 354–62.

27. See Dieter Mehl, *The Middle English Romance of the Thirteenth and Fourteenth Centuries*, p. 4; Charles Moorman, *A Knyght There Was*, p. 59; Benson, *Art and Tradition*, p. 244; Benson has since changed his view of chivalry's decadence, as he demonstrates in *Malory's* Morte Darthur, pp. 137–62; Broes, "*Sir Gawain and the Green Knight*," p. 54; John M. Ganim, "Disorientation, Style, and Consciousness in *Sir Gawain and the Green Knight*," *PMLA* 91 (1976): 377; Halpern, "The Last Temptation of Gawain," pp. 353–84.

Sir Gawain and the Green Knight demands that its fictitious readers respond not to a single view but to the wide range of chivalric expression found in contemporary texts. The narrator speaks as both a promotor and a detractor of chivalry. Furthermore, diverse responses to chivalry are dramatically realized. The Green Knight expresses the critical challenge offered by moralists; Bertilak's wife operates according to a literal interpretation of French romance; the two courts practice chivalry primarily as a social code; and Gawain exemplifies an idealistic, self-conscious ethical version. The central conflicts in *Sir Gawain and the Green Knight* resonate against the different value systems invoked.

The various evaluations of Gawain's actions encourage readers to look critically at the hero, yet at the same time much of the action is presented from Gawain's point of view, enabling us to identify with him. Through his consciousness readers are initiated into the experience of being a knight. Although other characters may not appreciate the rigorous idealism of his self-definition, extratextual sources identify his intricate synthesis of knightly virtues as one of the many versions of fourteenth-century chivalry. Gawain's quest dramatizes the tensions inherent in conforming to chivalric ideals. Sir Gawain defines his public personality in his pentangle version of chivalry. The pentangle represents an elaborate ethical code by which the hero must continually measure his behavior. Challenges to Gawain's self-definition occur in the tests the plot poses. Like actual fourteenth-century knights, he must maintain the image which his coat of arms proclaims for him, constantly proving his reputation. Writings by medieval knights illuminate the poem because they bring into focus Gawain's struggles.

A major problem Gawain faces in *Sir Gawain and the Green Knight* is his confrontation with his own mortality. Here again, fourteenth-century sources augment our understanding of the hero's dilemma, for in responses to death the tensions between Christianity and chivalry appear most marked. Medieval texts and artefacts relating to death bring into sharper relief the problems with which Gawain struggles.

13

CONCEPTS OF CHIVALRY

Although reading *Sir Gawain and the Green Knight* with a sense of its historical milieu goes against the classicist habit of universalizing literature,[28] an awareness of other fourteenth-century expressions of the problems the poem entertains can only deepen readers' understanding. By drawing attention to significance which might otherwise be missed, extratextual sources enable modern readers to assume more self-consciously the roles the poem assigns.

Since the linear unfolding of the poem's plot influences readers' perception of *Sir Gawain and the Green Knight*, I have chosen to discuss the poem fitt by fitt. However, in an attempt to prepare for the complexities I see in the poem, I preface my analysis with a consideration of the cultural context of *Sir Gawain and the Green Knight*. I examine the ethical system of chivalry, first as it is formulated in various texts and second as it is reflected in the writings of several fourteenth-century knights. I then discuss Christian and chivalric attitudes toward death. Having delineated conflicting fourteenth-century perceptions of knighthood and mortality, I return to the poem to show how the text challenges readers with its presentation of competing ethical systems.

28. The classicist approach to literature is attacked briefly by Robertson, *A Preface to Chaucer*, p. 3, and at greater length by Jauss, *Toward an Aesthetic of Reception*, pp. 13ff.

Chapter 2

Chivalry in the Fourteenth Century

n examination of fourteenth-century responses to chivalry reveals that unresolved tension is undeniably present in late-medieval culture. By the fourteenth century chivalry was described in a variety of ways.[1] Knighthood might be promoted as the flower of secular culture or vilified as a blemish on society. *Sir Gawain and the Green Knight* requires that its fictitious readers respond not to a single view but to the wide range of chivalric expression found in contemporary texts. To understand the poem more fully, modern readers need to recover the complex awareness of chivalry that *Sir Gawain and the Green Knight* demands.

Huizinga's vision of knighthood's decadence in the later Middle Ages still holds sway among scholars of medieval literature. Raymond Kilgour presents the case against chivalry most emphatically, citing the works of medieval critics of knightly behavior as evidence that the forms of chivalry no longer corresponded to reality.[2] Most of the studies of *Sir Gawain and the Green Knight* that consider chivalry reflect the theory of its decadence

---

1. Using some of the sources I shall refer to, John Barnie illustrates the range of opinion on war from the period 1337–99; John Barnie, *War in Medieval Society*, pp. 56–96.
2. Raymond L. Kilgour, *The Decline of Chivalry*.

15

and view the poem as a testament to that vision of medieval history.[3]

In Huizinga's powerful depiction of the late Middle Ages, chivalry is a romantic fiction masking actions which evince "more of covetousness, of cruelty, of cool calculation, of well-understood self-interest, and of diplomatic subtlety, than of chivalry."[4] From the vantage point of one who knows what follows, Huizinga discounts chivalry as a flamboyant anachronism:

Towards the end of the period our attention is almost entirely occupied by the genesis of new forms of political and economic life (absolutism, capitalism), and new modes of expression (Renaissance). From this point of view feudalism and chivalry appear as little more than a remnant of the superannuated order already crumbling into insignificance, and, for the understanding of the epoch, almost negligible.[5]

Although this statement dismisses those features of late-medieval society that do not foreshadow subsequent developments, the "remnant of the superannuated order" is precisely what fascinates Huizinga. Addressing the fact that medieval chronicles and literature frequently convey a sense of chivalry's importance, Huizinga argues that long after nobility and feudalism were important factors in society they still exerted force in the minds of the people. Thus chivalric rituals, symbols, and ideals were sensed as powerful despite their discordance with reality. Viewing history as an evolutionary continuum, Huizinga emphasizes knighthood's decay, yet his work attests to late-medieval society's fascination with chivalry.[6]

3. See chap. 1.
4. J. Huizinga, *The Waning of the Middle Ages*, p. 67.
5. Ibid., pp. 56–57.
6. In his study of fifteenth-century England, Arthur B. Ferguson considerably refines Huizinga's theories. He suggests that in the fourteenth century there was still some correspondence between chivalric concepts and political reality. Moreover, he argues that concurrent with the decline of knighthood's military function in the fifteenth century was the transformation of chivalric ideals into the notion of the Tudor gentleman-governor. Arthur B. Ferguson, *The Indian Summer of English Chivalry*.

Recently historians of medieval knighthood have attacked Huizinga's argument, offering evidence for chivalry's vital role in medieval war, politics, and society. Michael Powicke documents an increase in the status of knights, citing sumptuary laws and the inauguration of secular chivalric orders.[7] Gervase Mathew argues that knightly ideals were essential to the development of the ethical standards of late-medieval aristocrats.[8] Juliet Vale convincingly documents the significance of the Order of the Garter in Edward III's French campaigns.[9] Malcolm Vale's study of fifteenth-century knighthood refutes Huizinga's assertion of chivalry's negligible importance in late-medieval institutions with evidence of the continuing military prestige of knights.[10] Maurice Keen's investigation of chivalry undermines Huizinga's theory by demonstrating the many ways in which the institution flourished in the later Middle Ages.[11] He argues that knightly ideals served not to mask the realities of life but to oppose them.[12] In concluding his study, Keen becomes an apologist for chivalry, proposing that its ideals of honor, nobility, courtliness, and personal integrity not only inspired medieval Europeans but also remained a legacy for subsequent centuries of Western civilization.[13]

Implicit in the theory of late-medieval decadence is the assumption that in past centuries chivalry was a more vital ethical system. History offers little evidence for such a conclusion. Keen convincingly argues that the age of chivalry spans the years from about 1100 to the beginning of the sixteenth century.[14] Sidney Painter identifies chivalry's golden age as the fourteenth cen-

7. Michael Powicke, *Military Obligation in Medieval England*, p. 172.
8. See Gervase Mathew, "Ideals of Knighthood in Late Fourteenth Century England," in *Studies in Medieval History Presented to F. M. Powicke*, pp. 354–62; and Gervase Mathew, *The Court of Richard II.*
9. Juliet Vale, *Edward III and Chivalry*, pp. 76–91.
10. Malcolm Vale, *War and Chivalry.*
11. Maurice Keen, *Chivalry.*
12. Ibid., p. 237.
13. Ibid., pp. 249–53.
14. Ibid., pp. 1, 18–43.

tury.[15] Arthur Ferguson recognizes the same period as the time when the ethical code of chivalry was known by knights who still had practical military significance.[16] Nonetheless, throughout the Middle Ages moralists insisted on the diminished virtue of their knightly contemporaries, comparing them for didactic purposes with exemplars from the past. In the twelfth century Peter of Blois contrasted the sottishness of contemporary knights with the discipline of Roman soldiers.[17] Throughout the thirteenth, fourteenth, and fifteenth centuries preachers looked back on a golden age of chivalry and saw their own age as decadent.[18] Since medieval writers located the inception of chivalry in the distant biblical or classical past,[19] the moralist argument for a golden age was not easily refuted.

Twentieth-century views of chivalry from Huizinga to Keen demonstrate the range of opinion found in the original sources, for when historians argue either for knighthood's decadence or for its vitality, they adopt positions taken by medieval writers. In documenting the vitality of chivalry as a military ideal, recent studies correct a deficiency in Huizinga's influential theory of knighthood's decadence in the later Middle Ages. Nevertheless, they understate chivalry's moral elements, minimizing the importance of Christian ideals in knightly practice.[20]

Sir Gawain and the Green Knight reflects the range of perspective available to readers in fourteenth-century England. From the scant evidence that remains in wills and accounts, it appears that the libraries of fourteenth-century aristocrats reflected a variety of subject and style.[21] A range of diverse texts, including sermon,

---

15. Sidney Painter, *French Chivalry*.
16. Ferguson, *The Indian Summer of English Chivalry*, pp. 111–12.
17. Kilgour, *The Decline of Chivalry*, pp. 4–5.
18. G. R. Owst, *Literature and Pulpit in Medieval England*, pp. 331–32.
19. See Keen, *Chivalry*, pp. 102–24.
20. See Keen's conclusions in ibid., p. 199.
21. For a summary of various sources see V. J. Scattergood, "Literary Culture at the Court of Richard II," in V. J. Scattergood and J. W. Sherborne, eds., *English Court Culture in the Later Middle Ages*, pp. 29–43; and Elizabeth Salter, *Fourteenth Century English Poetry*, pp. 19–51.

treatise, and romance, mediated the medieval experience of chivalry. In addition, in a culture where art was integral to daily life, iconographic representations cannot be ignored.[22] Although some sources reflect a uniform approach to chivalry, others display a conscious effort to synthesize conflicting cultural ideas. Still others consciously or unconsciously include views that are diametrically opposed. The images of knighthood experienced by late-medieval readers can be divided broadly into romance, heraldic, and moralistic views. *Sir Gawain and the Green Knight* dramatizes the tensions in chivalry by bringing together these conflicting visions.

The Romance View

The most readily apparent approach to chivalry reflected in *Sir Gawain and the Green Knight* is the romance view. Unlike heraldic and moralist productions, romances do not usually pretend to mirror reality accurately. Since the world of romance belongs to fairy tale and magic,[23] location in time and place is relatively unimportant. Structure is related to narrative themes, rather than to chronology or cause and effect. In the common theme of the testing of the hero, the ordeals are often unmotivated.[24] Nonetheless, however remote from reality it may be, romance offers an image of medieval knighthood.

In the self-defining quests of romance heroes projections of knightly ideals can be seen. Romances are vehicles for the demonstration of a range of chivalric virtues: prowess, piety, loyalty, mercy, and courtesy. In fictional form they delineate the knightly

22. Salter, *Fourteenth Century English Poetry*, pp. 4–5.
23. Erich Auerbach, *Mimesis: The Representation of Reality in Western Literature*, trans. W. A. Trask, p. 113.
24. For example, in *Sir Gawain and the Green Knight* the plot is explained unsatisfactorily and in retrospect as Morgan la Faye's scheme to destroy Guinevere and discredit Bertilak's court; see Morton D. Bloomfield, "Episodic Motivation and Marvels in Epic and Romance," in *Essays and Explorations*, p. 109.

qualities that chivalric treatises anatomize. While invariably illustrating the hero's prowess, romance quests demonstrate additional virtues. The grail romances reveal the exemplary piety of their heroes. In many romances, *Sir Gawain and the Green Knight* included, an essential chivalric attribute is fidelity to one's word. *Amis and Amiloun* dramatizes how a pledge made between two friends transcends attachments between husbands and wives, fathers and sons. In love romances the knight's fidelity to his mistress is often tried, perhaps by the illusion of her death, as in *Cliges*, or perhaps by the temptations of beautiful women. The knight's courtesy to all women might be assayed by the introduction of suppliants unrelated to the quest. A number of these delay Launcelot in *Le Chevalier de la Charette*, giving him the opportunity to demonstrate his proper knightly deference to anyone female. Heroes can also demonstrate their knightly excellence by granting their opponents their lives. The chivalric trait of mercy is so important that it often goes against what is practical, for example, when Launcelot spares the troublesome Meleageant in *Le Chevalier de la Charette*. *Sir Gawain and the Green Knight* exemplifies the romance's capacity for exploring chivalry in the exploits of individual heroes, for Gawain continually strives to adhere to the cluster of chivalric qualities signified in his heraldic emblem.

Besides celebrating individual chivalry, romance promotes courtly society. Descriptions of feasts, jousts, and courtly manners dominate romance texts. Though superficially the leisure pastimes of aristocratic society, they carry profound significance. The feasts and games of romance celebrate medieval civilization — the culture's mastery of the primal drives of appetite, sexuality, and aggression. Moralists attempted to curb these drives through abstinence, chastity, and crusade. A secular counterpart to such religious formulations, the romance embodies control in the rituals of feasting, courtly love, and the joust. All are games in the broadest sense, governing impulse with fixed rules and elevating primal urges to the plane of art.[25] In sublimating basic

25. See Huizinga's discussions of play in *Homo Ludens* and in *The Waning of the Middle Ages*.

20

desires and fears (the desire for food and sex, the fear of death) these forms assert the superiority of civilized over primitive man or knight over churl.

Where fabliau characters are concerned with the swift gratification of physical impulses, the heroes and heroines of romance protract or defer the consummation of physical acts. In *Sir Gawain and the Green Knight*, Arthur follows his custom of delaying the holiday feast until he hears a tale or witnesses a joust. In many romances where knights of similar status do battle, the satisfaction of killing the opponent is rejected in favor of a more civilized act of mercy. In *Le Chevalier de la Charette*, once it is clear that Launcelot has the upper hand, Meleageant is rebuked by his father for continuing the fight. His wish to battle to the death is seen as improper, a breach of chivalric decorum, for he wants to move from a game of aggression to the brute fact. In romances whose central theme is love, lovers are usually denied the solace of each other's presence for much of the time and must be content with adoring each other from afar. Some obstacle, such as a noble husband, a tyrannical relative, or even the lovers' own innocence, impedes the course of their affair.

In the central role that it allows women, romance differs notably from other expressions of chivalry familiar to aristocrats. Women represent much more than the object of knightly passion. A scene from Geoffrey of Monmouth's *Historia Regum Brittanniae* shows a celebration at Camelot where ladies watch from the castle walls as knights joust below. Military prowess is essential if the knights are to win feminine approval, for the ladies refuse anyone who has not proved himself three times in war: "nullius amorem habere dignabantur nisi tercio in milicia probatus esset."[26] Here women do more than observe knights: they also judge them. As early as Chrétien de Troyes, woman's role as arbiter of knightly deeds is fully developed. Though the knight usually rides out alone, the court and particularly the lady

26. Geoffrey of Monmouth, *Historia Regum Britanniae*, ed. Acton Griscom, pp. 457–58.

draw him back for judgment and approval. In *Le Chevalier de la Charette* witnesses to the hero's actions are omnipresent and are often female. The knight's own lady is usually central judge and witness, however. Even when Guinevere is absent, as in the episode when Launcelot is asked to mount the cart, she is somehow observing and evaluating his actions.

The women of courtly literature have been described as projections of man's image or desires,[27] but this view overemphasizes woman's passivity. While the lady's function as mirror to the knight may constrain her, at the same time it empowers her. She may be inactive or even physically confined, as is Guinevere in *Le Chevalier de la Charette*, but as a judge of chivalry she also exerts control. In *Sir Gawain and the Green Knight*, Bertilak's wife exploits her power as judge, refusing to reflect back the image of pentangle chivalry that Gawain expects.

Although romance presents an idealized picture of chivalry, it is by no means uncritical. The amalgam of virtues belonging to knighthood is scrutinized as early as Chrétien and exposed as a fragile synthesis. Although love and prowess typically complement each other, in some of Chrétien's romances they are temporarily at odds. Maintaining honor requires a knight's constant activity, but love draws him away from military action. In *Erec et Enide* the hero invites criticism when he abandons himself to enjoying his wife. Enide's shame at the withdrawal of social approval compels Erec to reassert his prowess. In *Yvain* the opposite happens, and the hero neglects his lady in the interest of winning a reputation in tournaments.

The tension between honor and love becomes irreconcilable in *Le Chevalier de la Charette*. Launcelot's consuming adoration of Guinevere enables him to endure gladly situations which bring him dishonor in society. Launcelot hesitates for only a few paces, debating about the shame which he will incur, before he leaps into the executioner's cart in obedience to love's commands:

27. Joan Ferrante, *Woman as Image in Medieval Literature*, p. 95.

N'est pas el cuer, mes an la boche,
Reisons qui ce dire li ose
mes Amors est el cuer anclose
qui li commande et semont
que tost an la charrete mont.
Amors le vialt et il i saut
que de la honte ne li chaut
puis qu'Amors le comande et vialt.[28]

The division between *Reisons* and *Amors* illustrates the extreme nature of Launcelot's passion and seems to imply criticism.[29] Launcelot becomes almost puppetlike in his capitulation to love. The internal rhyme of *vialt* and *sault* makes the hero seem mechanical for a moment and therefore comic.

If Chrétien's chivalric romances expose tensions in knighthood, the Vulgate cycle of the thirteenth century portrays romance chivalry as finally irreconcilable with religious ideals. Conventional romance heroes like Gawain become foils to the ascetic knights of *La Queste del Saint Graal*. In contrast to Galahad — the perfect model of knighthood — Gawain is "serjanz mauvés et desloiaux."[30] Because Gawain will not submit to the rigors of penance, he violates the loyalty he owes to God. Launcelot admits to having served the enemy of his true lord. He characterizes his past career of love and prowess, the one celebrated in secular romances, as the broad way to destruction:[31] "Et si me sui ocis en la voie que len troeve au comencement large et enmielee: ce est li comencemenz de pechié."[32] Since Launcelot is

28. Chrétien de Troyes, *Le Chevalier de la Charette*, ed. Mario Roques, lines 370–77 ("Reason, who dares to say this to him, does not move the heart, but only the mouth. But enclosed in the heart is Love, which commands and incites him to quickly get up on the cart. Love desires it, and he jumps in, for shame matters not to him since Love commands and desires it").

29. A similar opposition between reason and love exists in *Le Roman de la Rose*.

30. *La Queste del Saint Graal*, ed. Albert Pauphilet, p. 52 ("wicked and disloyal servant").

31. See Matthew 6:13–14.

32. *Graal*, p. 65 ("And I have destroyed myself in the way that one finds at first broad and honeyed: that is the beginning of sin").

23

not as recalcitrant as Gawain, he achieves limited success on the quest. Nonetheless, progress depends on his renouncing his worldly attachment to Guinevere, even though it has made him a hero.

By the end of the fourteenth century chivalric romance possesses a rich literary history. Some, like *Havelock* and *King Horn*, are uncritical celebrations of the individual excellence of the hero. Others, like Chrétien's, affirm chivalric culture even as they explore the tensions inherent in knightly ideals. Still others graft the moralist condemnation of secular chivalry onto the romance form, contrasting the flaws of conventional heroes with the purity of knights like Galahad. *Sir Gawain and the Green Knight* is the heir of a complex tradition capable of reflecting varied images of chivalry.

The Heraldic View

A second view of chivalry helpful in understanding *Sir Gawain and the Green Knight* is the heraldic perspective. Though modern readers may be familiar with romance, the significance of heraldry is largely lost to them. Nonetheless, the texts, iconography, and customs of heraldry are part of *Sir Gawain and the Green Knight*'s intertextuality. An understanding of heraldic ideology opens up more interpretative possibilities in the poem.

A work which demonstrates heraldic values is *The Siege of Caerlaverock*, a poem describing the capture of Caerlaverock castle by Edward I in 1300.[33] The poem celebrates uncritically

---

33. N. Denholm-Young suggests that the poem may be the last example of the union of the herald and minstrel professions. N. Denholm-Young, *History and Heraldry: 1285 to 1310*, p. 60. Though it does not contain blazon per se and thus is not relevant to Denholm-Young's concerns, the Chandos Herald's poem suggests that a continuing literary tradition among heralds should not be ruled out. Moreover, Keen mentions the literary accomplishments of two late-fourteenth-century heralds, Claes van Heynen, the Gelre Herald, and the Austrian Peter Suchenwirt. Keen, *Chivalry*, pp. 139–40.

the values of the military elite. While much of *The Siege of Caerlaverock* lists the battalions of the English army in the manner of rolls of arms, the poem's elaboration of armorial material demonstrates its ideology. After mentioning the occasion of the battle, the poem describes the visual spectacle of the assembled army: "La ot meint riche guarnement / Brodé sur sendaus et samis, / Meint beau penon en lance mis, / Meinte baniere deploié."[34] These lines recognize the element of pure display in armorial bearings. Much more than simple marks of recognition, their lavish decoration suggests that they are marks of status. Like romance, heraldry celebrates the spectacle of aristocratic life.

The heraldic concern with individual prowess is apparent in *The Siege of Caerlaverock*. Battle descriptions concentrate on personal feats as though other facets of military action are unimportant. When knights distinguish themselves by *faits d'armes*, their insignia are recorded, as though deeds of military prowess validate the posession of armorial bearings.

In *The Siege of Caerlaverock* arms convey more than rank and class. As in *Sir Gawain and the Green Knight* they can be read as symbols of individual integrity. In the description of Edward I heraldry fuses with characterization:

> En sa baniere trois lupart
> De or fin estoient mis en rouge
> Courant, feloun, fier e harouge.
> Par tel signifiance mis
> Ke ainsi est vers ses enemis
> Li rois fiers, felons, e haustans,
> Car sa morsure ne est tastans
> Nuls ke ne en soit envenimez
> Nonporquant tost est ralumez
> De douce debonaireté

34. *The Siege of Caerlaverock*, ed. Gerald J. Brault, in *Eight Thirteenth Century Rolls of Arms in Anglo-Norman Blazon*, lines 18–21 ("There were many rich ornaments embroidered on silks and satins, many fine pennants fixed on lances, many banners displayed").

CONCEPTS OF CHIVALRY

Kant il requerent se amisté
E a sa pais veullent venir.[35]

Here we see the herald as exegete, insisting that insignia are not simply marks which distinguish one knight from another but that they bear moral significance too. Heraldic manuals of the fourteenth and fifteenth centuries develop this aspect of the science, offering detailed interpretations of the marks and colors of coats of arms.[36]

The Chandos Herald's *La Vie du Prince Noir*, like *The Siege of Caerlaverock*, exemplifies the heraldic view of chivalry. Overwhelmingly, the biography is a military record, frequently reminiscent of rolls of arms. It contains little about the Prince in any capacity other than knight. *La Vie du Prince Noir* begins by comparing Edward to Claruz, Caesar, and Arthur.[37] Next the biography gives the prince's parentage, a pedigree appropriate to a fighter:

Filtz au noble roi Edward
Qui n'avoit pas le coeur coward
Et filtz Phelippe la roigne
Qe fuist la parfite racine
De toute honour et de nobletée
De sens, de valoir et de largetée.[38]

Edward's military qualities need no elaboration and are therefore expressed in a brief negative statement. The Queen's description,

35. *Caerlaverock*, lines 220–31 ("On his banner were three leopards of fine gold on a ground of red, courant, savage, fierce, and arrogant, placed to show this meaning, that thus toward his enemies the king is fierce, cruel and haughty. For none taste his bite who are not poisoned by it. Nonetheless all are soon revived with sweet gentleness when they seek his friendship and wish to come to his peace").

36. See Evan Jones, *Medieval Heraldry*.

37. Chandos Herald, *La Vie du Prince Noir*, ed. Diana B. Tyson; the notes to lines 51–52, p. 167, identify Claruz as the king of India, a major character in the *Voeux du paon*.

38. Ibid., lines 57–62 ("Son to noble King Edward who had no coward heart and son of Philippa the queen who was the perfect root of all honor and nobility, of understanding, valor, and largesse").

which one might expect to contain conventional remarks on physical beauty, emphasizes instead her suitability as the breeder of military heroes. Each of the adjectives applied to Philippa, with the possible exception of the ambiguous *sens* which can mean feeling as well as judgment, apply to the martial virtues of chivalry. The lack of attention given gentler qualities such as courtesy or pity distinguishes the herald's perspective from the romancer's.

Though the military perspective dominates, *La Vie du Prince Noir* does not completely ignore religious and courtly versions of chivalry. A brief character sketch of the Prince unites the three ideologies in a single exemplary figure:

> Coment il fuist, c'este chose clere,
> Si pruys, si hardy, si vaillant,
> Et si curtois et si sachant
> Et si bien amoit seinte Esglise
> De bon coer, et sur tut guise
> La tres hauteine Trinitée.[39]

Here military prowess unites with courtliness and piety, synthesizing the different currents of chivalry. The poem occasionally shows these virtues in action. In scenes with Joan of Kent, the Prince is attentive, loving, and courteous (lines 2072–88, 3769–72). Praying before a battle, he appears pious (lines 1263–73, 3174–83), and in attributing his success to God, he demonstrates humility (lines 1428, 3503).

Nevertheless, the purely military aspects of the Prince's life dominate the biography. The only parts which depart from the general and conventional are the descriptions of campaigns. In concluding, the Chandos Herald excuses the brevity of the book, and explains the narrative's selectivity:

39. Ibid., lines 82–87 ("What he was is a plain fact, so worthy, so hardy, so valiant, so courteous and so wise, and he gladly loved Holy Church so well, and in every way the most high Trinity").

Mais pur doner en remembrance
De son fait et reconissance
Et de sa tres haute proesse
Et de sa tres noble largesse
Et auxi de sa prodhommie,
Comment il fu tut sa vie
Prodhomme loialx et catholiqes
Et en touz biens faire publiqes
Et si ot si tres noble fin.[40]

This statement encapsulates the book's heraldic ideology. In the biography language is comparable to heraldic iconography, serving as *remembrance* of deeds of arms and *reconissance* of those qualities which define nobility. The portrait offered in final tribute to the Black Prince emphasizes his military chivalry. *Proesse* and *largesse* have primary importance although, finally, the perspective broadens to embrace the moralist vision of the knight's social and moral responsibilities. Having honored his obligation to God and society, the Prince makes a noble end, remembering God and demonstrating exemplary humility in accepting death.

In the heraldic perspective external actions, not inner motives, determine knightly excellence. Nobility is seen not as a static quality but as one which must be maintained through action. Heraldic insignia testify to the ongoing chivalric practices of the bearers. Arms are dishonored or withdrawn for unchivalric actions such as treason, cowardice, or breach of faith.[41] Coats of arms can also be amended to reflect the altered status of the bearers. Edward III proclaimed his interest in the French throne by placing the fleurs-de-lis in the first and fourth quarters of his shield.[42] Changes can also reflect honors won. A heart was added

40. Ibid., lines 4101–4809 ("But to commit to memory and recognition his most superior prowess and his most noble largesse and also his worthiness, for all his life he was a worthy man, loyal and catholic, and manifest in doing good; and so he made a very noble end").
41. Keen, *Chivalry*, pp. 174–76.
42. C. Wilfred Scott-Giles, *The Romance of Heraldry*, pp. 97–98.

to the Douglas shield to reflect the service that Sir James Douglas reportedly performed in carrying the embalmed heart of Robert Bruce to the Holy Land.[43] Gawain's adoption of first the pentangle and then the girdle as personal symbols illustrates the dynamic nature of heraldic emblems.

An understanding of heraldry offers insight not just into local details of *Sir Gawain and the Green Knight* but also into broader problems of interpretation. A heraldic reading of *Sir Gawain and the Green Knight*, not being concerned with niceties of conscience, would affirm the hero's excellence without qualification. Such might be the view of Arthur and his court, as they make light of the hero's moral transgressions, boldly adopting the green baldric in an assertion of the excellence of their fraternity.

Moralist Views

The writings of moralists offer another ideological perspective which informs the fourteenth-century experience of chivalry. In *Sir Gawain and the Green Knight* the moralist influence is seen in the hero's spiritual idealism as well as in narrative comments and imagery. Moralist views of chivalry are not uniform but range from condemnation to praise. It should be noted that moralist perspectives do not predominate in *Sir Gawain and the Green Knight*; rather they balance other versions of chivalry.

In its extreme the moralist's social vision is pessimistic, for man's efforts achieve only evil.[44] The era of harmony depicted in Chaucer's poem "The Former Age" depends on human inaction (lines 21–24):

> No ship yit karf the wawes grene and blewe;
> No marchaunt yit ne fette outlandish ware;

43. Ibid., pp. 83–84.
44. See William J. Brandt's analysis of the *Gesta Stephani* in *The Shape of Medieval History*, pp. 76–78; Brandt concludes that "the natural and normal state was always the preexistent ground; action was a disturbance of the norm, an unnatural state of affairs" (p. 79).

No trompes for the werres folk ne knewe,
Ne toures heye and walles rounde or square.[45]

The series of negatives condemns the glories of aristocratic culture — the lavish art, costume, and architecture — the achievements of the merchant and military classes. Everything that heralds and romancers celebrate is here condemned as a token of man's fall from grace. The poem ends with no redeeming vision but an image of the present as "nis but covetyse, / Doublenesse, and tresoun, and envye, / Poyson, manslauhtre, and mordre in sondry wyse" (lines 61–63). The poem offers no suggestions for reform, only a lament on the degraded state of humanity.

A less pessimistic view of knighthood is found in the popular fourteenth-century treatise *L'Arbre des Batailles*, by Honoré Bouvet.[46] Unlike "The Former Age," Bouvet's treatise does not depict war as an unfortunate disruption. Quite the contrary, the first part of the book discusses the inevitability of war and even its divine sanction. The book's concern is to reform the laws of war and promote their enforcement. The appeal of Bouvet's work to lords, knights, and heralds is not surprising in that it popularizes the work of Italian legists[47] and, in part, addresses the need for codification of chivalric practices.[48]

Although Bouvet's treatise fulfills a need for the military aristocracy, it demonstrates the antichivalric bias characteristic of much moralist writing. For example, the last chapter defines the virtuous king as one who exercises *measure*: "And it is a thing by

45. Geoffrey Chaucer, "The Former Age," in *The Works of Geoffrey Chaucer*, ed. F. N. Robinson, 2d ed., p. 534.
46. Until fairly recently the author of this treatise was known as Bonet. For a brief discussion of the emendation of his name see N. A. R. Wright, "The *Tree of Battles* of Honoré Bouvet and the Laws of War," in C. T. Allmand, ed., *War, Literature, and Politics in the Late Middle Ages*, p. 12 n. 2.
47. See ibid., pp. 25–26.
48. Expressed by Geoffrey de Charny in his *Demandes* to the Order of the Star; by Thomas, duke of Gloucester, in his treatise on the manner of combating within the lists; and by the production of heraldic manuals in the late fourteenth century (see Jones, *Medieval Heraldry*).

no means unfitting for a prince to be measured in his eating and his drinking, and in his clothing, and in hearing minstrels, fawners, and flatterers with the tongue, for to give his goods to such people is pains thrown away."[49] Although he attacks courtly practices, Bouvet blunts the criticism with the qualification, "I do not say however that a prince should not have such people, and confer benefits on them without excess."[50] His recommendations for the conduct and diet of a knight evoke a conventional comparison of former heroes with decadent contemporaries:

The chivalry of today is by no means of the valor of former times, for according to the old laws knights ate beans and bacon and coarse meats; they lay hard and wore harness most of the time; they dwelt outside cities and liked the air of the open country and willingly kept the field; and they did not usually dispute as to which was the best wine but drank clear water, because they could endure all hardship and labor.[51]

Looking back to a classical golden age of chivalry, Bouvet embraces Roman ideals of discipline imported from Vegetius. Although incompatible with the practices of medieval knights, Roman definitions of soldiery held considerable authority since knights traced their origins to the Roman republic and beyond.[52]

A moralist alternative to condemnation was the attempt to reform knighthood through spiritual inspiration. While Bouvet sought to better society by imposing the order of law on its military class, the church promoted crusading as a means of redeeming the military aristocracy's violence and corruption. Despite ever-diminishing success, the ideal persisted in the fourteenth century.

One of the attractions of crusading was that it reconciled the conflicting demands of military and religious chivalry, offering an arena for displays of prowess and promising honor, wealth,

49. Honoré Bouvet, *The Tree of Battles of Honoré Bonet*, trans. G. W. Coopland, p. 213.
50. Ibid.
51. Ibid.
52. Wright, *"The Tree of Battles,"* pp. 27–29.

and salvation. Despite the disastrous failure of the Battle of Nicopolis in 1396, the crusading ideal did not die. Henry V seems to have kept alive his crusader father's dream of regaining the Holy Land for Christianity. He died regretting that he did not live to rebuild the walls of Jerusalem.[53]

Reviving the Crusades was a lifelong ambition of Philippe de Mézières, a counselor of Charles V until the king's death in 1380. In 1395, Philippe addressed a letter to Richard II, eloquently depicting his hopes for a lasting peace with France, an end to the papal schism, and a united crusade. He describes the situations in need of reform as three wounds that afflict the whole of Christendom. The letter contains a conventional attack on the evils of war. It portrays society's upheaval and knighthood's flagrant abandonment of its obligations to the church, women, widows, and orphans. This part of Philippe's argument echoes the moralist analysis of social chaos as proceeding from knighthood's violation of its social responsibilities. Subsequently, however, the letter offers a vision of hope, for the kings of England and France are to be the balm and lodestone that help heal society's wounds.

Philippe imagines a future in which there is fraternal harmony between the nations and a revival of the military and religious virtues of past heroes:

Et quant a doulce compaignie en fait d'armes, voire encontre les anemis de la foy, l'un de vous ii. soit Rollant le vaillant et l'autre soit le tres debonnaire Olivier.

Mais quant a magnificence royale et imperiale, l'un de vous ii. soit par imitacion les tres vaillant et tres preux Charlemaine, et l'autre soit le tres excellent et tres preux roy Artus, c'est assavoir contre les anemis de la foy, contre les scismatiques et hereges.[54]

53. K. B. McFarlane, *Lancastrian Kings and Lollard Knights*, p. 125.
54. Phillipe de Mézières, *Letter to Richard II*, trans. G. W. Coopland, p. 144; all translations are from this edition ("As regards companionship in arms against the enemies of the Faith, let one of you be the noble Roland and the other the very perfect Oliver; and in the matter of royal and imperial splendour, one of you may imitate the very bold and excellent King Arthur, when you fight against the enemies of the Faith, against schismatics and heretics" [p. 70]).

The letter promotes a spiritualized chivalry where the two Christian kings settle disagreements armed with "l'escu de doulce pacience...et du haubert de liberalite."[55] Although this vision is consistent with the moralist position, it is better attuned to the aristocratic point of view than is Chaucer's poem or even Bouvet's treatise. In fact, it grafts onto the moralist position elements from the aristocratic genres of romance and heraldry. In referring to legendary heroes of the past and allegorizing articles of armor, Philippe appropriates symbols rich in meaning for the knightly class.

A highly influential fusion of moralist and aristocratic values is found in Raymon Lull's *Le Libre del Orde de Cavalleria.* Until a vision of the crucified Christ inspired him to become a missionary to the Saracens, Lull was a worldly courtier. His father was a distinguished knight, a seneschal at the court of James II of Aragon.[56] Imbued with the values of the medieval aristocracy, Lull writes as an insider seeking to define and elevate the tenets of chivalry.

The popularity of Lull's work in the fourteenth and fifteenth centuries indicates that he mirrors the knightly class as it would like to be seen. A. T. P. Byles lists ten extant manuscripts of the fourteenth and fifteenth centuries in which the work appears. In addition, in the fourteenth century D. Juan Manuel appropriated Lull's treatise in "Le Livre du Chevalier et de l'Ecuyer," while Johanot Martorell made considerable use of it in his romance "Tirant le Blanc."[57] Lull's treatise appears in several manuscripts containing other works of interest to a great lord. British Museum Royal Manuscript 14E.ii includes *L'Ordre de Chevalerie* in a handsome collection compiled for Edward IV.[58] One manuscript of the late fourteenth century contains other didactic works of

---

55. Ibid., ("the shield of [sweet] patience...and the hauberk of generosity").
56. A. T. P. Byles's introduction to Ramon Lull, *The Book of the Ordre of Chyualry* trans. William Caxton, p. xi. All quotations from Lull are taken from this edition, since the language is more accessible than the original Catalan.
57. Ibid., p. xv.
58. Ibid., p. xviii.

interest to a knight: "Le Romance de Melibee et Prudence," "Traite Politique sur les Devoirs respectifs de Princes & des Sujets" (the pseudo-Aristotelian *Secretum Secretorum*), "Les Romanes des 7 Sages," and a French version of the story of patient Griselda.[59] An early-fifteenth-century manuscript combines Honoré Bouvet's *L'Arbre des Batailles* with Lull's treatise.[60]

Like Philippe de Mézières, Lull frames his program for reform in terms that would appeal to aristocrats. The treatise on chivalry begins like a romance. In a forest by a fair fountain a young squire meets an old hermit, who sighs at the mention of chivalry and gladly responds to the squire's request for instruction. The hermit is a former knight who "fledde the world / by cause that the feblenesse of his body in the whiche he was by old age fallen" (p. 4). His present state is by no means a rejection of his past, for he daily contemplates "the grace and bounte / that god hath gyuen and done to me in this world / by cause that I honoured and mayntened with al my power thordre of Chyualrye" (p. 11). Here Lull anticipates Malory's synthesis of secular and religious chivalry in the final book of the *Morte D'Arthure*. In describing Launcelot's last adventures, Malory adds material which reconciles the *Mort Artu's* separation of love and prowess from penitence and spirituality.[61]

Lull's treatise seeks to reform knights by identifying nobility with virtue. More than an occupation, chivalry involves the commitment to a moral code far more rigorous than that required of ordinary men. While the knight is expected to be physically fit and adept at hunting and tourneying, at the same time, he is called on to exercise moral virtues: "justice / wysedom / charite loyalte / verite / humylite / strength hope swiftnes & al other vertues semblable" (p. 31). Unless a knight practices these virtues, the hermit claims, he is "more vyle than the smythe or the carpenter that done their offyce after that they owe to doo & have

59. Ibid., p. xvi.
60. Ibid., p. xvii.
61. Benson, *Malory's* Morte D'Arthure, pp. 223–34.

lerned" (p. 24). Lull makes moral excellence the characteristic which distinguishes knights from men of inferior social status.

In granting knighthood superior status, *Le Libre del Ordre de Cavalleria* offers a picture of society that would be attractive to an aristocratic audience. In his account of the origins of chivalry Lull asserts that the knight's place in society is his reward for his inherently superior qualities: "At the begynnyng whan to the world was comen mesprysion / justyce retorned by drede in to honour in whiche she was wonte to be / And therefore alle the peple was deuyded by thousandes / And of eche thousand was chosen a man moost loyal / most stronge / and of most noble courage / & better enseygned and manerd than al the other" (p. 15). The false etymological association of *miles* ("knight") and *mille* ("thousand") suits the hermit's rhetorical purpose, for subsequently he exhorts the squire to remember the noble origins of the order and to see that "the noblesse of his courage in good custommes accorde to the begynnynge of chyualry" (p. 16).

The hermit augments the moral status of the knightly order by comparing it to the priesthood. The rituals described as appropriate to the knighting of a squire recall those for taking holy orders. The night before his ordination the squire confesses his sins and keeps a vigil through the night, fasting and praying. In the morning he attends a mass at which he swears "to keepe thonour of chyualry with al his power" (p. 67). At the ceremony a priest gives a sermon about the twelve articles of the faith, the Ten Commandments, and the seven sacraments as well as the other things pertaining to chivalry. Like ecclesiastical vestments, knightly armor is given spiritual significance. The sword symbolizes the Cross, which defeats enemies of heaven; the spear symbolizes truth; the helmet, modesty; the habergeon, a fortress against vice. The symbolic interpretation even extends to the horse and all its equipment. In synthesizing knightly and clerical rituals and symbols, Lull attempts to reform chivalry by offering it an attractive, spiritualized definition of itself.

Although necessarily selective, this discussion of moralist depictions of chivalry suggests the diversity of opinion current in the fourteenth century. While generally agreeing that the present state of affairs is unsatisfactory, moralist views range from Lull's approving portrayal of knighthood as a beneficent force in society to the negativism of "The Former Age," where the possibility of reform is not considered. Reformers might exhort knights to return to earlier standards, as does Honoré Bouvet, or, in the manner of Lull, promote an idealized image of chivalry. Finally, in assuming that readers share a concern with the state of chivalry, most of these texts argue against a simplistic notion of chivalric decadence.

Even if moralizing were not balanced against romance and heraldic perspectives in *Sir Gawain and the Green Knight*, the range of moralist opinion on chivalry would require that modern readers exercise caution in assigning any particular attitude to the poem. As it is, *Sir Gawain and the Green Knight* contains a number of perspectives which reflect romance, heraldic, and moralist texts. The multiple points of view are suspended in a way that enables each to challenge the other. No single view dominates unequivocally in this indeterminate poem. Thus, readers are provoked into evaluating each view and thereby gaining a broader understanding of chivalry.

Chapter 3

The Knight's Experience of Chivalry

s I shall show in my analysis of the poem, the hero of *Sir Gawain and the Green Knight* defines his vocation in terms of religious, military and courtly ideals, synthesizing the modes of chivalry current in the fourteenth century. The poem dramatizes Gawain's discovery of the tensions inherent in his personal ideology and the difficulties in following it. In confronting the complexities of fourteenth century knighthood, *Sir Gawain and the Green Knight* offers a more profound view of knighthood than is found in most chivalric texts. The knights of both moralist and heraldic texts tend to be one-dimensional figures. Although the Chandos Herald characterizes the Black Prince, like Gawain, as an amalgam of religious, courtly, and military virtues, the heraldic narrative avoids discussing the Prince's internal conflicts. Many romances, though concerned with their heroes' inner lives, avoid dealing with the complexity of knightly ideals. By contrast, texts written by fourteenth century knights indicate the pressures of living according to an ideology that was defined in various, contradictory terms. Though the number of extant examples is small, texts containing elements of knightly autobiography reflect the conflicts presented in *Sir Gawain and the Green Knight*. These knightly productions suggest that the chivalric ideals in the poem are not old-fashioned but are integral to fourteenth-century aristocratic experience.

A text which addresses the various definitions of chivalry, recognizing all of them as imperatives for the ideal knight, is the fourteenth-century *Le livre Messire Geoffroi de Charny*. Its author, Geoffroi de Charny, was one of the most famous knights of his century, celebrated for his bravery and nobility.[1] In Froissart's heraldic portrayal of his death, he fights bravely in the press at Poitiers, always near King John, dying with the French standard in his hands. In contrast to the external view found in Froissart's *Chroniques* is the image of knighthood conveyed by Geoffroi's book. *Le livre Messire Geoffroi de Charny* examines moralistic, heraldic, and romance visions of chivalry, demonstrating the practical difficulties in upholding knightly ideals.

The framework of Geoffroi's book reflects the influence of moralistic definitions of chivalry. Like Lull, Geoffroi addresses young men desiring instruction in knightly practices, identifying knighthood and priesthood as the two noble professions in society. Geoffroi's view of chivalry differs from Lull's in replacing abstractions with realistic details which depart ironically from the idealized formulations of *Le libre del Orde de Caballeria*.

Geoffroi's consideration of practical details such as the expense of knightly equipment and the discomfort of campaigns distinguishes his treatment of chivalry from more conventional versions. Though the book often affirms the knightly profession, it also characterizes knighthood as a life devoid of glamor:

> Or vois tu dons
> Que asne qui runge chardons,
> Ne beste qui trait en limons,
> Si com me semble,

---

1. Geoffroi de Charny is responsible for two other chivalric texts: a list of questions addressed to the knights of Notre-Dame de la Noble Maison and a prose work on chivalry, *Le livre de chevalerie*, ed. Kervyn de Lettenhove, in *Oevres de Froissart*, 1: 463–533.

THE KNIGHT'S EXPERIENCE OF CHIVALRY

N'ont pas tant de male meschance
Com cil qui en armes s'avance.[2]

Comparisons between knights and ignoble beasts of burden counter the elevated status claimed for chivalry from the outset, drawing attention to the discrepancy between ideals and experience.

At times Geoffroi's book affirms the heraldic view of knighthood by implying that *faits d'armes* are good in themselves. The book ends on that positive note, urging young readers to joust and tourney "pour cognoissance, / Et pour la guerre."[3] The places knights seek out to win prowess are portrayed as stages for the display of chivalric virtues:

Et s'illec vas,
Honneur, bonté y trouveras,
Prouesce, vaillance y verras,
Et courtoisie,
Hardiesce si n'i faut mie,
Loyauté y maine grant vie,
Et puis largesce.[4]

The list mentions the virtues celebrated in heraldic texts and romances, for when Geoffroi speaks in general terms, he echoes the abstractions found in these two aristocratic literary forms.

Surprisingly, Geoffroi's book also at times reflects a moralist perspective. His depiction of the knight as lover does not follow the romance *topos* in which the hero's prowess comes from his

2. Geoffroi de Charny, "Le livre Messire Geoffroi de Charny," ed. Arthur Piaget, *Romania* 26 (1897): 403 ("Well you see that neither the ass who eats thistles nor the beast who pulls in harness, so it seems to me, has as much misfortune as he who takes up arms").
3. Ibid., p. 409 ("for recognition and for war").
4. Ibid., pp. 409–10 ("And if you go there, you will find honor and goodness; you will see prowess, valour and courtesy, no less than boldness, loyalty leads a grand life there, and then largesse").

desire to win his mistress. Instead, Geoffroi's knight performs haphazardly, sometimes jousting well but sometimes achieving nothing and appearing foolish in front of his lover. The speaker rejects the romance topos for a Boethian view of temporal life governed by inconstant fortune:

> Un autre jour tu jousteras bien,
> A l'autre tu n'en feras rien.
> Scez tu pour quoy?
> Que tu n'es pas sire de toy,
> Mais Dieu, qui fist et toy et moy;
> Si te pren garde
> Que tu te mettes en sa garde,
> Ne de lui servir ne te tarde,
> Bien t'est mestier.[5]

Pious refrains reappear throughout the book, offering an image of celestial stability when other visions of life fail.

Although Geoffroi's book employs heraldic, romance, and moralist perspectives, attempts to depict knightly experience in detail diverge from standard formulations. Chivalry loses some of its glamour in Geoffroi's description of the discomforts knights must endure in the quest for honor. Expeditions "oultre la mer" are depicted as long, arduous, and terrifying for men with no experience in seafaring. Even provided one arrives at his destination safely, the horses are likely to be out of condition after the long journey. Geoffroi describes the physical discomforts of traveling and making war that are missing from idealized depictions by heralds and romancers. Details such as these lead Piaget to conclude: "Son livre est vécu. Il est précieux en ce qu'il met sous nos yeux, incomplètement et maladroitement peut-être, l'état d'âme d'un chevalier du XIVe siècle."[6]

5. Ibid., p. 400 ("One day you joust well, on another you do nothing. Do you know why? Because you are not lord of yourself, but God, who made both you and me takes heed of you. So you should put yourself in his care and not put off being his servant, for truly he is your master").
6. Ibid., p. 410.

THE KNIGHT'S EXPERIENCE OF CHIVALRY

Geoffroi's description of the terror experienced in battle re-creates for modern readers an experience seldom expressed in romance or heraldry:

> Paour te faut avoir souvent
> Quant vois tes ennemis devant
> Vers toi venir,
> Lances bessiees, pour toy ferir,
> Les espees pour revenir
> Toi courre sus;
> Garros, quarriaux te vienent sus;
> Tu ne scez duquel tu dois plus
> Ton corps garder.[7]

In this realistic depiction of combat the knights's vulnerability comes across clearly, as readers are asked to envision innumerable hostile objects hurtling toward them and to imagine the resulting feelings of helplessness. As Geoffroi evokes the carnage of battle, asking readers to see the corpses strewn around, he suggests an alternative to death:

> Mès tes chevaux n'est mie mors,
> Bien puet aler;
> Par lui ton cors pourras sauver,
> Sanz honneur t'en pourra mener.
> Se tu demeures,
> Honneur en avras toutes heures,
> Se tu fuis, tu te deshonneures.
> N'est ce (grant) martire?[8]

The question which punctuates this scene — whether death in battle is not a great martyrdom — might seem ironic, but subse-

7. Ibid., p. 401 ("You must often feel fear when you see your enemies coming toward you, lances lowered to strike you, swords ready to return and fall upon you. Spears and arrows fall on you and you do not know against which you should more defend your body").

8. Ibid., pp. 401–402 ("But your horse is not dead yet; he can go well. Through him you can save your skin, he can lead you away without honor. If you stay you will always have honor; if you flee, you will dishonor yourself. Is this not a great martyrdom?").

quent lines affirming chivalry as "Le plus noble mestier a droit / Et le plus perilleux"[9] suggest that the lines should be read literally. Geoffroi transforms a hopeless situation into a redemptive experience by conflating religious and chivalric honors. In doing so, he imitates the rhetoric used by advocates of crusading.

A rather inconsistent attitude toward knighthood emerges from Geoffroi's book. At times abstractions promoting chivalry appear unquestioned, while in other instances they are undercut by realistic details which portray the knight as a man struggling with mundane physical necessities. Although the book frequently insists that all good comes from God, sometimes this moralistic perspective gives way to more exclusively aristocratic sentiments about chivalry. The speaker appears to be struggling with conflicting cultural definitions of his profession. His allegiance shifts from a moralistic view of man as powerless without God's grace to a heraldic view of the knight as noble exemplar. Like *Sir Gawain and the Green Knight*, *Le livre Messire Geoffroi de Charny* contains conflicting views of chivalry; however, the English poem has better control of these warring elements, since it expresses contradictory attitudes through different characters.

Though different from Geoffroi's book, a text by Henry Grosmont, duke of Lancaster, one of Geoffroi's English contemporaries, offers insight into fourteenth-century chivalric conflicts. Like Geoffroi de Charny, Henry of Lancaster was a well-respected knight. Froissart describes him as "si bon chevalier et si recommandé," "moult noble et très gentil de coeur," "aimé de tous ses amis, et ressoingné de tous ses ennemis."[10] In contrast to this idealized figure stands the self-portrait in Henry's *Le livre de seyntz medicines*, a book of personal meditation and confession written in 1354. Henry's book differs from Geoffroi's in addressing readers as Christians rather than as knights. One of his

9. Ibid., p. 402 ("The noblest profession indeed, and the most dangerous").

10. Jean Froissart, *Les chroniques de Sire Jean Froissart*, ed. J. A. C. Buchon, 1: 14, 186, 194 ("such a good knight and so highly commended," "most noble and very gentle of heart," "loved by all his friends and respected by all his enemies").

avowed purposes is "pur moustrer apertement a toutz gientz la malviesté q'est en moy, de qoi jeo me confesse a Dieux et a tout le monde."[11] Following a convention of manuals such as the *Liber poenitentialis*,[12] Henry examines all his senses for traces of each of the deadly sins. Fulfilling the expectations of the genre, Henry accuses himself of transgression in every instance. Nonetheless, despite its conventionality, *Le livre de seyntz medicines* dramatizes the conflict between orthodox Christianity and the chivalric life.

Le livre de seyntz medicines evaluates in a penitential context the career presented heraldically in Froissart. As Henry reviews his life from the perspective of a Christian seeking heavenly, not worldly, glory, his prowess becomes pride and his fame, vanity:

Jeo pensai qu jeo ne resemblai mye as autres, mes qe jeo les passai touz de force, de hardement, de sens, de poair; et de toutes altres choses me [sembloit] qe jeo sur touz les fesoie [mens] al poynt. Et tout ceo cy et uncore asseez plus m'est issuz par la bouche et mult sovent.[13]

Concern with personal reputation and accomplishments, acceptable in romance and heraldry, translates into mortal sin in this confessional context. Interestingly, Henry does not deny his exceptional qualities—his strength, agility, beauty, stature, and nobility—for he sees them all as virtues and graces which God has given him to save his soul, and which, ironically, he has misused to his mortal peril. Henry's self-criticism recalls the charges of the hermit to Launcelot in *La queste del Saint Graal*. While the holy man grants that Launcelot is an exceptional knight, he regrets that the hero abuses his gifts by serving the devil.

In *Le livre de seyntz medicines* a moralist version of the self

11. Henry of Lancaster, *Le livre de seyntz medicines*, ed. E. J. Arnould, p. 240 ("to show everyone the evil in me which I confess to God and the whole world").

12. See discussion in Mary Flowers Braswell, *The Medieval Sinner*, pp. 33–60.

13. Henry of Lancaster, *Le livre de seyntz medicines*, p. 16 ("I thought that I did not resemble others at all, but that I surpassed them all in force, hardiness, in understanding, in power; and in all other things, it seemed to me that I was above them all in all respects. And all this and still more issued from my mouth and very often").

opposes the heraldic and romance emphasis on individual prowess. In Henry's pathology of vice the etiology of many of his sins lies in his placing himself, not God, at the center of the universe. Although all sinners might be charged with this fault,[14] the knight is particularly vulnerable, for romance and heraldry promote individualism as part of chivalry.

Henry confesses to many sins committed in the interest of increasing his knightly status. Instead of loving his companions in arms, he envies them, slandering them to promote himself. Acts which might easily be praised by heralds become reprehensible in a penitential context. Henry admits to sins of wrath in exhorting his men to acts of manslaughter and violence, "sovent sanz en avoir bone discrecion de droit ou nule."[15] Though chivalric manuals justify acts of violence committed in a just cause, Henry regrets all his violent deeds, remembering Christ's command that people love one another. As a penitent he feels that he inverted Christian values when he was a knight. Ironically, in taking his enemy's life, he risked eternal death, "la mort d'enfern."[16]

As a penitent Christian, Henry renounces a number of aristocratic practices. Feasting, celebrated in romance as the mastery of instinct, becomes for Henry an occasion for sin. Where romance emphasizes visual spectacle and culinary refinement, the penitent dwells on excess:

Bien sovent me sui mellez, come d'aler par grant delite la ou jeo ai quidee de trover les bons gras morceaux et les bons vyns; et ja n'estoient mes pieez

14. In a discussion of thirteenth-century penitential theology, Braswell makes the following distinction between saint and sinner: "The will of every true Christian is inclined toward the Divine Will, or the *bonum in communis*. And once it espouses this common good, it ceases striving for those things forbidden to it. The sinner, on the other hand, shuns the common good for his own *individual* good—he is an egotist; therefore he chooses evil, and, in doing so, he isolates himself from those around him." Braswell, *The Medieval Sinner*, p. 33.

15. Henry of Lancaster, *Le livre de seyntz medicines*, p. 17 ("often without having good judgment of the good, or none at all").

16. Ibid., p. 18.

ne ne sont si prestes de moy servir a mon profite come a mon damage: c'est a entendre q'ils ne sont mye si apparaillez ne si prestes de moi reporter ariere come ils sont d'aler la, car si plein est lui cheitife corps de viande, et si esturdie de boire est la test, que les pieez ont nul poair de faire lour office.[17]

Henry portrays himself as a grotesque figure, a moralist's version of the glutton. Nonetheless, he acknowledges another view and admits its validity, "Pur ceo n'est pas qe les seignurs et altres solonc lour estat q'il ne covigne faire si comme a lour estat demande: mesque ceo saroit par atant passer, bien serroit."[18] In attempting to reconcile the opposition between romance and moralist ideologies, Henry distinguishes between behavior appropriate to his class and that which is excessive. The disparity between penitential and romance points of view provokes the qualification, for both ideologies form part of Henry's experience as a knight.

Another clash of ideologies takes place in Henry's confession of lechery, for he condemns acts which romances idealize. He regrets sending messages to his mistress, pleading, "'Jeo ne su qe mort, si vous ne me eidetz.'" This hyperbolic claim, so familiar to readers of love poetry should be reworded according to the penitent Henry: "'Jeo ne su qe mort, si vous m'eideteitz' deusse jeo dire pur dire voir; et ensi va le mien amy, qe poi d'amisté me fait et se va perdre et moi ausint."[19] Subsequently Henry renounces the practice of singing love songs because they have led himself and others to sin. Other courtly practices such as jousts

17. Ibid., pp. 75–76 ("Often I was stirred to go for great delight where I sought out fine rich morsels and good wine; and already my feet were not so quick to serve me to my profit as to my detriment: that is to say that they were and are never as ready nor as nimble to take me back as they are to go there, for my worthless body is so full of meat, and my head is so full of drink, that my feet have no power to do their office").

18. Ibid., p. 20 ("For this is not to say that lords and others according to their estate should not do as their estate demands but that is acceptable in measure and would be fine").

19. Ibid., pp. 21–22 ("'I will die if you help me,' ought I to say to speak truly; and that goes for my friend, who does me little kindess and will lose herself and me too").

and dances provided Henry with occasions for temptation. Nonetheless, he insists that one can attend such affairs without committing sin: "Et ceo si die jeo puisse avoir tout fait ceo q'est dit devant, com en jouster, en daunser et en autres choses de qoi le piee se melle, sanz pecché, sicom jeo espoire qe tout pleyn d'autres fount et poent bien faire."[20] Although embracing orthodox Christianity, Henry stops short of condemning aristocratic practices. He modifies the moralist position by condemning his own frailty, not the weakness of the whole class.

Finally Henry partly reconciles Christianity and chivalry by casting Christ as his feudal lord. His sinfulness represents a violation of his fealty to his sovereign: "Et jeo lui riens sa curtoisie mult vileynement, sa largesce mult escarcement, et toutez ses bontés mult tresmalement."[21] As a sinner Henry has joined the devil's party, a breach of faith which he also describes in chivalric terms: "A celui qui serroit a vous contraire: c'est a l'ord deable d'enfern, et non pas soulement de sa liveree, mes [de] sa propre seutte comme compaignon."[22] Employing the language and symbols of knighthood in a religious context, Henry of Lancaster embraces a spiritual version of chivalry which recalls *La queste del Saint Graal*. Religious and secular practices stand in conflict, the latter offering more temptations than the weak-willed penitent can withstand. Henry embraces religious chivalry and prays for the strength to overcome his weaknesses. Nonetheless, his class affiliations prevent him from condemning secular chivalry as wholeheartedly as the Grail romance does.

The books by Geoffroi de Charny and Henry of Lancaster represent some attempt to reconcile conflicting versions of chivalry. Other partly autobiographical knightly productions are less

20. Ibid., p. 78 ("And that is to say that I could have done all that which I spoke of before like jousting, dancing, and other things that the feet are involved in without sin, as I fully hope others do and are well able to do").

21. Ibid., p. 116 ("And I reward his courtesy most churlishly, his largess most sparingly, and all his bounties most unfairly").

22. Ibid., p. 3 ("He who would be opposed to you is of the order of the devil in hell, and not only of his livery, but of his own acquaintance as a companion").

equivocal in their rejection of romance and heraldic values. In a book written for the instruction of his daughters about 1372, the Knight de la Tour-Landry also addresses the tension inherent in chivalric ideals. The Prologue tells how the knight composed his book with the assistance of two priests and two clerks. The book strongly reflects clerical influence, particularly in the host of moral examples it offers in the style of the sermon. For the most part the book imitates antichivalric moralists in denouncing knighthood.

When the Knight de la Tour Landry entertains heraldic and romance points of view, he does so only to discredit them more persuasively. The impetus to compose an instructional treatise for his motherless daughters comes from the author's memories of how "my felawes comened with ladies and gentil-women."[23] As a father he is suspicious of all protests of love, and he remembers his fellows as false to a man. Nonetheless, he portrays himself holding the opposite point of view in a discussion about love which took place before his wife's death:

Lady, why shalle not the ladyes and damoysels loue peramours? For in certayne, me semeth that in good loue and trewe, maye be but welthe and honour, and also the louer is the better therfore, & more gay and Ioly; and also the more encouraged to exercyse hym self more ofte in armes. And taketh therfore better maner in al estates, for to please vnto his lady or loue. And in lyke wyse dothe she of whome he is enamoured, for to please him the better, as ferre as she loueth hym.[24]

The knight's argument derives from the standard romance theme of love's power to elevate and ennoble its practitioners. To counter her husband's argument, the Lady de la Tour-Landry offers a description of chivalric practice that recalls Henry of Lancaster's confession:

23. Knight of La Tour-Landry, *The Book of the Knight of La Tour-Landry*, ed. Thomas Wright, p. 2. Subsequent references are to this edition.
24. Ibid., pp. 171–72.

these wordes coste to them but lytyll to say, for to gete the better and sooner the grace and good wylle of theyr peramours. For of suche wordes and other moche merueyllous, many one vseth full ofte; but how be hit that they saye that "for them and for theyr loue they done hit," In good feyth they done it only for to enhaunce them self, and for to drawe vnto them the grace and vayne glory of the world.[25]

The lady challenges romance ideology, claiming that, like extravagant protests of love, the knightly pursuit of glory is motivated by self-interest. Her charges contain elements of practical common sense as well as conventional Christian morality. She cautions her daughters to love honorable men, but not "to be so ferforth enamoured, in soo moche that this loue be mayster of her, and maketh them to falle in somme fowle and shamefull delyte."[26] She reasons that a lady needs to preserve her good name against slanderers and backbiters and that excessive love for a paramour detracts from the worship of God. She also argues that many men deceive women with false protests of love and boast of it afterward to their friends, while a true lover is much more reticent in the presence of his lady. Her advice is for women to hold back until marriage, as many men lose interest in their paramours and never propose. The only acceptable relationship with a man other than her husband is one which excludes physical contact. While echoing the clerical view of the conflict between human and divine love, her advice has the practical tone of a mother who wants her daughters to marry sensibly. Her discussion includes cautionary examples of women whose forwardness discouraged suitors and of those who threw themselves away on married men, priests, or social inferiors.

In a book that is overwhelmingly composed of rather crude moral exempla, this vignette of aristocratic parents debating the romance view of love and prowess offers a welcome relief. Although there is little tension in the debate, the lord clearly offering an argument which he subsequently rejects, the scene

25. Ibid., p. 172.
26. Ibid., p. 173.

48

suggests that the conflicting points of view were part of contemporary cultural experience.

Contrasting arguments about love and chivalric prowess are set forth in *The Boke of Cupide*, a courtly poem attributed to John Clanvowe. In the poem a nightingale and a cuckoo debate the nature of love. The nightingale offers the romance argument that love ennobles its practitioners:

> ffor therof truly cometh al goodnesse,
> Al honour and al gentilnesse,
> Worship, ese, and al hertys lust,
> Perfyt ioy and ful ensured trust,
> Iolite, plesaunce and freshenesse,
>
> Lovelyhed and trewe companye,
> Semelyhed, largesse and curtesie,
> Drede of shame and forto don amys
> ffor he that truly loues seruaunt ys,
> Wer lother to be schamed then to dye.[27]

The nightingale's litany of virtues is familiar to readers of romance. In answer, the cuckoo has a corresponding list of love's evil effects:

> For loving is in yonge folke but rage,
> And in olde hit is a grete dotage,
> Who most hit vseth, most he shal apeyre.
>
> For ther of cometh disese and heuynesse,
> Sorow and care and mony a grete seknesse,
> Dispite, debate, angre, and envye,
> Repreve and shame, vntrust and ielosye,
> Pride and myschefe, pouert and wodenesse.[28]

---

27. Sir John Clanvowe, *The Boke of Cupide*, ed. V. J. Scattergood, in *The Works of Sir John Clanvowe*, lines 151–60.
28. Ibid., lines 168–75.

Although the dreamer takes the nightingale's part, the cuckoo's argument troubles him. He routs the cuckoo with a stone, but he does not resolve the disparity between the two points of view.

While the attitude toward romance ideology is ambiguous in *The Boke of Cupide*, it is transparently negative in *The Two Ways*. The latter work, more certainly attributable to Sir John Clanvowe, is a prose treatise on the quest for salvation. Its title comes from Christ's description of the narrow gate to salvation and the broad road to destruction. Readers of *La queste del Saint Graal* might be reminded of Launcelot's description of his chivalric career as the way to destruction. The treatise opposes the transience of mortal life to the permanence of heaven and in doing so implicitly rejects human attachments: "ffor al þe ioye of þis world is passynge, and soone ydoon, and foule ymedled with dreede and with manye ooþer diseesis and travailles."[29] The only love the treatise speaks of is proper Christian love for God and for one's neighbor, all other attachments are characterized as "flesshly lustes" or "lykerousnesse."

The Two Ways goes on to reject the glorification of prowess characteristic of romance and heraldic literature. Like *La queste del Saint Graal*, the treatise distinguishes between worldly and spiritual values:

...ffor þe world holt hem worsshipful þat been greete werreyours and fiȝteres and þat distroyen and wynnen manye loondis, and waasten and ȝeuen much good to hem þat haan ynouȝ, and þat dispenden oultrageously in mete, in drynke, in clooþing, in buyldyng and in lyuyng in eese, slouþe and many ooþere synnes. And also þe world worsshipeþ hem muchel þat woln bee venged proudly and dispitously of euery wrong þat is seid or doon to hem. And of swyche folke men maken bookes and soonges and reeden and syngen of hem for to hoolde þe mynde of here deedes þe lengere heere vpon eerth, ffor þat is a þing þat worldely men desiren greetly þat here naame myghte laste loonge after hem heere vpon eerth.[30]

29. John Clanvowe, *The Two Ways*, ed. V. J. Scattergood, in *The Works of Sir John Clanvowe*, lines 29–33.
30. Ibid., lines 484–99.

Contemporary aristocratic literature, such as Froissart's chronicles or the Chandos Herald's biography of the Black Prince, celebrates activities which *The Two Ways* condemns as destruction and waste. Unable to reconcile secular chivalry with spiritual purity, *The Two Ways* renounces it completely. To live simply, away from "swich forseid riot, noise, and stryf" is to incur the scorn of the world which "hooldeþ hem lolleris and loselis, foolis and schameful wrecches."[31] The treatise congratulates those who defy convention and choose the narrow way, for "God holdeth hem moost wise and most worsshipful."[32]

It would be a distortion to suggest that all knights possessed a high degree of awareness about themselves and their profession. Many knights would have been minimally concerned with chivalric ideals. One of these is the Bascot de Mauléon, a Gascon freebooter whose reminiscences Froissart records. For him the wars with France had more to do with profit than chivalry: "J'ai aucune fois été rué jus, tant que je n'avois sur quoi monter; à l'autre fois riche assez, ainsi que les bonnes fortunes venoient."[33] His preoccupation with profit makes him sound startlingly callous when he tells of the death of his commander, Sir John Aimery. Guichard Albregon, one of the count of Sancerre's men, had taken the wounded commander prisoner and left him at an inn with the request that his valuable acquisition be cared for. After telling of the setback he and his company suffered, the Bascot de Mauléon turns to the fate of his commander: "Toutefois Guichard Albregon perdit son prisonnier, car cil à qui il l'avoit enchargé par sa grand' mauvaiseté et negligence, le laissa tant saigner que il en mourut. Ainsi fina Messire Jean Aymery."[34] The

31. Ibid., lines 505, 512–13. Scattergood points out that "the word *loller* meaning 'loafer' or 'idler' was often deliberately or scornfully misapplied to Lollards" (p. 20).

32. Ibid., lines 513–14.

33. Froissart, *Les chroniques de Sire Jean Froissart*, 2: 114 ("Sometimes I've been in such a state that I didn't even have a mount; at other times, quite rich when good fortune came my way").

34. Ibid., p. 410 ("Anyway, Guichart Albregon lost his prisoner because the man with whom he left him let him bleed to death through his great wickedness and negligence. That was the end of Sir John Aimery").

words are shocking because they contrast with Froissart's customary manner of reporting death with either a commentary about the loss to society or a eulogy for the man. The Bascot de Mauléon's identification with the knight who has lost a considerable ransom takes precedence over any finer sentiments.

The Bascot de Mauléon seems remarkably free of guilt over any violations of chivalry he may have committed. He boasts of his capture of the castle of Thurie, a feat accomplished through trickery rather than prowess. The freebooter's one commitment seems to be to the king of England, his feudal lord. He tells of the many who have died in battle, and of one who changed to the French side and concludes, "je demeurai bon Anglois et se serai tant comme je vivrai."[35] The Bascot de Mauléon does not possess the developed conscience that Lull hopes for in a knight; nonetheless, he seems aware of loftier standards than his, and wants his loyalty to be a matter of record.

In the records left by these very different fourteenth-century knights, we see a wide variety of responses to the chivalric profession. Geoffroi de Charny embraces it while acknowledging its hardships; Henry of Lancaster sees it as fraught with moral hazards for a man of his particular composition and tries to avoid its temptations; Sir John Clanvowe completely rejects its values; the Knight de la Tour-Landry recognizes that its doctrines of love and prowess threaten the well-being of his daughters; the Bascot de Mauléon enjoys its opportunities while blithely ignoring its ideals.

In the course of each individual's life experiential reality interacts with received wisdom and leads to the adoption of a personal philosophy which tries to accommodate both. The Bascot de Mauléon chooses to respect his feudal obligation of loyalty and to disregard further elaborations of the chivalric code. The responses of the other knights are more complex. The Knight de la Tour-Landry deeply mistrusts his peers' ability to uphold chivalry's tenets, and he adopts both pragmatic and moralistic ap-

---

35. Ibid., p. 410 ("...I remained a good Englishman, and I will as long as I live").

proaches to chivalry. While Henry of Lancaster describes an uneasy tension between the temptations of his knightly life-style and his Christian obligations, Sir John Clanvowe sees the same problem as an irreconcilable conflict. Geoffroi de Charny accepts the marriage of religion and chivalry, taking comfort in the belief that God, "qui fait tout par raison," lends order to his turbulent experience. In each instance the disparity between idealistic abstractions and perceived reality forces the writer to attempt to resolve the tensions by adopting a particular stance.

Sir Gawain and the Green Knight imaginatively re-creates for its readers the conflicts experienced by fourteenth-century knights in their practice of chivalry. The various roles readers are asked to adopt engage them in the problems the poem entertains, encouraging active involvement in the interpretive process. But for original readers who were in fact knights, *Sir Gawain and the Green Knight* would assume added meaning, for it dramatizes conflicts that formed part of their lived experience. For those readers, interpreting the poem would augment their understanding of their own lives.

Chapter 4

Attitudes Toward Death
in the Fourteenth Century

n *Sir Gawain and the Green Knight* the hero's confrontation with what seems an inescapable death is of central importance. Readers would be sensitized to the prominence of the theme of mortality, for images of death permeate the medieval world. Twentieth-century readers can adopt the consciousness the poem demands only by examining the cultural milieu of its fictional readers.

Nowhere is the tension inherent in conflicting attitudes to knighthood more apparent than in fourteenth-century responses to mortality. Moralist and aristocratic attitudes toward death differ markedly. Fourteenth-century knights find themselves in a paradoxical situation when seeking the proper response to death. The warrior code calls on them to defy death in acts of heroism and thereby gain worldly fame. Christianity warns them to reject worldly things and to accept death as the passage from this imperfect world to eternity. Finally, chivalry demands that knights somehow reconcile these opposing responses.

Although knights are thoroughly instructed in orthodox Christian theology, they inherit values older than those embraced by the Church, which makes the adoption of an orthodox Christian response to death problematic. Chivalry began in the struggle for power in a warrior society, and it incorporates into its ethos the ancient, heroic defiance of death. In war and tournament, resplendent in armor and heraldic emblems, the knight challenges death. As the representative of his culture's heroic ideal, he wins respect by risking his life. Either by dying bravely or by defeating his opponent, the knight gains worldly reputation and the symbolic victory over death. To achieve honor among his peers, the knight has to overcome his Christian consciousness of the inevitable triumph of death and the consequent worthlessness of worldly attainment.

The old warrior attitude toward death is dramatized in Froissart's depiction of the last hours of the earl of Douglas. The chronicler tells how, when the Scots were beginning to lose ground at Otterburn, the earl rushed into the press with a battle-ax, clearing the way before him with mighty blows like another Hector. Froissart depicts the mortally wounded earl making a final speech which beautifully expresses the heroic attitude to death: "Loué en soit Dieu! On a de mes ancesteurs peu trouvé qui soient morts en chambre ni sus lit. Je vous dis, pensez de moi venger, car je me compte pour mort; le coeur me défaut trop souvent. Gautier, et vous Jean de Sain-Clar, redressez ma bannière et criez Douglas!"[1] The ethos embraced here is not that of the Church but the more ancient warrior code in which honor and vengeance are paramount. The earl's insistence on revenge directly opposes the Christian virtue of forgiveness. For him consolation comes from the knowledge that his followers will continue the fight. Their loyalty ensures the earl's immortality, as they take up his banner and his battle cry against the enemy.

The medieval heroes celebrated in heraldic literature stand out from ordinary men in their ability to put aside their instinctual fear of death. The Chandos Herald defines the heroic pose expected of knights in his account of the battle in which Sir William Felton was killed. One of the combatants was Raoul de

---

1. *Les chroniques de Sire Jean Froissart*, 2: 729 ("God be praised, one can find few of my ancestors who have died in chamber or bed. I ask you this: think of avenging me, because I count myself dead. My heart keeps failing so often. Walter, and you, John Sinclair, set up my banner again and cry Douglas!").

Hastynges, "qi la mort ne counte a deux gynges."[2] But most courageous was Sir William "le prus," who charged the enemy "comme homme sanz sens et sanz avis."[3] Both remarks suggest not an acceptance but a willful suppression of the painful reality of death that accompanied medieval warfare.[4]

Texts attempting to synthesize chivalry and Christianity often subscribe to a version of the warrior attitude toward death.[5] Ramon Lull places hardiness and courage among the highest of knighthood's virtues. To give in to fear is to be unchivalric:

Therfor he that more redoubteth or fereth the torment or peryll of his body than of his courage and vseth not thoffyce of Chyualrye / ne is not seruaunt ne obeyssaunt to other honoures / but is ageynste the ordre of chuyalrye whiche was bygonne by noblesse of courage.[6]

Although Lull does not deny the power of mortal terror, he insists that knights conquer fear with courage. Death in action brings great honor both to the individual and to the institution of knighthood: "And no man may more honoure and loue Chyualrye / ne more for hym maye not be do / than that deyeth for loue & for to honoure the ordre of chyualrye."[7] Like Lull, Geoffroi de Charny expresses the alternatives available very simply: flee and gain dishonor, or stay and have honor and martyrdom.[8] Geoffroi's choice of the word *martire* to describe the warrior's death reveals the element of denial in knightly bravery. To sacrifice one's life in some cause is seen as a transcendent experience which wins the knight immortality.

2. Chandos Herald, *La vie du Prince Noir*, line 2730 ("Who didn't set death at two cherries").
3. Ibid., line 2740 ("like a man without feeling or caution").
4. For a discussion of the numbers of fatalities in late medieval battles, see Keen, *Chivalry*, pp. 220–23.
5. The Grail romances, with their bias against martial action, are a notable exception.
6. Lull, *The Book of the Ordre of Chyualry*, p. 36.
7. Ibid., p. 37.
8. Quoted in chap. 3, above.

CONCEPTS OF CHIVALRY

In chivalric literature death in action has its consolations. In *The Knight's Tale*, Theseus finds redeeming value in Arcite's painful end: "And certeinly a man hath moost honour / To dyen in his excellence and flour, / Whan he is siker of his goode name; / Thanne hath he doon his freend, ne hym, no shame."[9] The ideal of honor lends significance to a death which would otherwise be brutal and meaningless.

The chivalric defiance of death seems to be recognized in the remarkable group of thirteenth- and fourteenth-century English tomb sculptures sometimes referred to as "dying Gauls."[10] Mainly from western England and the Midlands, these tombs differ from contemporary nonknightly funeral monuments in their intense "activation."[11] While ecclesiastical figures are almost invariably represented in tranquil poses, these knights are restlessly active. One of the finest examples of the activated knight is the late thirteenth century tomb sculpture in Dorchester Abbey, Oxon. Although the knight's head and feet are supported, the placement of the body, the flowing movement of the garments, and the pose of withdrawing sword from scabbard convey a sense of restless energy. The tomb in Exeter Cathedral believed to belong to Sir Richard de Stapleton shows the knight propped up with legs crossed, holding his shield and sword. A page at his feet leads a horse, while another page at his head is too badly damaged to interpret clearly. Hurtig, however, interprets the tomb as "an intense and eternal re-enactment of the experience of the battlefield."[12] In two midfourteenth-century Norfolk tombs at Ingham and Reepham,[13] the knights are in the act of withdrawing their swords as if challenging death rather than accepting it. Hurtig argues persuasively that these as well as the

9. Chaucer, *The Knight's Tale*, lines 3047–50.
10. Erwin Panofsky, *Tomb Sculpture*, ed. H. W. Janson, p. 56.
11. Judith Hurtig, *The Armored Gisant Before 1400*, p. 54. The term is borrowed from Panofsky, who applies it to Renaissance tomb sculpture. Hurtig argues that the vitality of these figures puts pressure on Panofsky's theory that the activation of the gisant is a Renaissance development. Ibid., p. 160.
12. Ibid., p. 157.
13. Ibid., p. 158.

Tomb Sculpture. Photo by Robert Clein. By permission of the Rector, Dorchester Abbey.

more passive tomb sculptures of knights which appeared in England and on the Continent should be seen as "commemorative" monuments expressing the worldly status of the knight.[14] Nevertheless, it is the peculiarly English development of the active knight which embodies best the cultural conception of the knight as death-defying hero.

Away from the battlefield the sports of fourteenth-century knights proclaim their defiance of death. The hunt, a favorite knightly occupation, is an elaborate and spectacular ritual in which the hunter demonstrates his control of life through stylized violence. The peacetime activities of jousting and tourneying — though conceived of as training for war — can be interpreted as aristocratic celebrations of life. Developments in armor and changes in the rules of play increased tournament safety in the later Middle Ages.[15] It became customary to celebrate royal births and marriages with lavish tournaments.[16] These games of aggression (often referred to as *hasti ludi*) embody knighthood's defiant pose.

The Christian attitude to death differs notably from the knightly approach. Christianity rejects the worldly glory sought by warriors, replacing it with the spiritual rewards enjoyed by the saints. The corporal relics of the holy come to symbolize the Christian victory of spirit over matter.[17] The endurance of the soul offers an escape from mortality that is more permanent and more widely accessible than that offered by earthly fame.

Rather than defying death, Christians accept it, making it an object of study. Contemplation of mortality leads to the recognition of the transitory nature of earthly things. Moralists turned various occasions into opportunities to reflect on death. John Mirk's sermon for the Feast of the Circumcision moves from

14. Ibid., p. 226. The term *commemorative* is taken from Panofsky, for Hurtig wishes to draw attention to "the medieval roots of what Panofsky has termed 'the resurgence of the commemorative point of view' in the early Renaissance."

15. Keen, *Chivalry*, p. 206.

16. See Vale, *Edward III and Chivalry*, pp. 57–75.

17. Peter Brown, *The Cult of the Saints*.

considering Christ's mortality to exhorting listeners to think on their own. Mirk's depiction of human life moves swiftly from the pain of birth to death, "for euermore, yn ych place, deth seweþ hym redy, forto falle on hym, what tyme, ny wher, he wot neuer."[18] In this sermon the purpose of meditation on personal mortality is to effect a spiritual circumcision, to "kytte away from hym þe lust of his flesche and worldes lykyng."[19]

Images of decaying human flesh provide the most dramatic examples of earthly transience. The corpse as memento mori appears early in a Christian context, transforming the Egyptian and Roman image from a carpe diem exhortation to an admonishment not to sacrifice eternal happiness for the fleeting pleasures of the body.[20] The image pervades the later Middle Ages. John Mirk's funeral sermon, "In die Sepulture Alicuius Mortui," takes the opportunity to remind listeners of their own mortality. It begins with the injunction, "Gode men, as ȝe alle se, here is a myrroure to vs alle: a corse browth to þe chyrch."[21] The corpse mirrors the audience's inevitable end, and Mirk describes its dissolution into "foulest careyn," cautioning each man and woman "þat is wyse, make hym redy þerto, for alle we schul dyon and we we wyte not how sone."[22] The message clerics preached was that men should confront their mortality to prepare for the realm beyond the grave.

Although the contempt for the flesh implicit in the memento mori symbol opposes the aristocratic view of life, the Black Prince chose a version of the motif for his own epitaph:

18. John Mirk, *Mirk's Festial*, ed. Theodor Erbe, p. 47.
19. Ibid., p. 47.
20. Versions of the motif are found in sixth-century Arabian poetry; see Kathleen Cohen, *Metamorphosis of a Death Symbol*, p. 21. Cohen cites examples beginning in the eleventh century, although she notes (p. 34 n. 38) that "Van Marle states that the inscription has occurred on Western tombs since the ninth century, but cites no early examples (*L'Iconographie de l'art profane*, La Haye, 1934, II, 384)." The image appears in a tenth-century Anglo-Saxon sermon in the Blickling Collection. *The Blickling Homilies of the Tenth Century*, ed. Rev. R. Morris, p. 113.
21. Mirk, *Mirk's Festial*, p. 294.
22. Ibid., p. 297.

Tu qe passez ove bouche close par la ou cest corps repose,
Entent ce qe te dirray, sicome te dire le say,
Tiel come tu es, Je autiel fu, tu seras tiel come je su,
De la mort ne pensay je mie, tant come javoy la vie.
En terre avoy grand richesse, dont je y fys grand noblesse,
Terre, mesons, et grand treshor, draps, chivalx, argent, et or.
Mes ore su je povres et cheitifs, profond en la terre gys,
Ma grand beaute est tout alee, ma char est tout gastee,
Moult est etroite ma meson. En moy na si verite non.[23]

The poem concludes with the appeal that the passers-by ask God for mercy on the dead man's behalf and with the hope that God will place those who pray for him in paradise, where none can be lowly (*cheitif*). With its reference to the worldly stature of the deceased, the poem is highly appropriate to the Black Prince; however, it is not original but is based on an anonymous thirteenth-century translation of the early-twelfth-century *Clericalis Disciplina* of Petrus Alphonsi.[24] Versions of the poem appear on other tombs, for example, those of John of Warenne, earl of Surrey (d. 1304), and Lord Robert Hungerford in Hungerford Church, Berkshire.[25]

To illustrate the impassive inevitability of death, moralists naturally turned to the figure which above all symbolized life for the Middle Ages: that of the chivalric youth. In didactic literature the knight's defiance of death is seen as blind folly. The King of Life in the incomplete morality *The Pride of Life* challenges

23. John Nichols, ed., *A Collection of All the Wills of the Kings and Queens of England*, pp. 67–68: "You who pass silently by where this body rests / Listen to what I say, for I tell you, / Such as you are, I once was, you will be what I am. / I did not think of death much while I had life. / On earth I had great wealth, from which I made great nobleness, / Land, houses, and great treasure, clothes, horses, silver and gold. / But now I am poor and lowly, laid deep in earth, / My great beauty is all gone, my flesh is all dissolved. / My house is very narrow and I have nothing but truth."
24. The author, who converted from Judaism to Christianity in 1106, was familiar with Arabic literature and probably derived the motif from that source. John Harvey, *The Black Prince and His Age*, p. 166.
25. Cohen, *Metamorphosis of a Death Symbol*, p. 69–70.

Death to fight against "me & my meyne / with fforce & armis."[26] Although the end of the play is missing, the King undoubtedly learns that man's inevitable fate is to die.

Although it is very late, a depiction which captures the irony of the medieval knight's heroism is Holbein's famous woodcut of the knight meeting death.[27] Attempting to defend himself, the knight, in full plate armor, brandishes his sword against the partly armed skeletal figure of Death. However, his bravery is to no avail against the force which levels all, for, unchivalrically, Death strikes him from behind.

One of the most powerful illustrations of the finiteness of human life, "The Legend of the Three Living and the Three Dead" dramatizes the conflict between the knight's and the Christian's experience of life. The motif began as a poem and eventually became popular as an isolated image. Illustrations always present a dramatic contrast between the elegantly aristocratic men representing the Three Living and the grotesquely decayed corpses of the Three Dead.[28] The legend shows that prowess, wealth, and status, so powerful in life, offer no consolation when man confronts his mortality.

"The Legend of the Three Living and the Three Dead" would undoubtedly be familiar to fourteenth-century English knights in either literary or iconographic form. A number of examples appear in mural paintings from parish churches. Moreover, the presence of the motif among the frescoes of the Great Chamber of Longthorpe Tower in Northamptonshire suggests that it may not have been unusual in a domestic context. Among the illuminated manuscripts containing the legend, a particularly relevant

26. Alois Brandl, ed., *The Pride of Life: Quellen des Weltlichen Dramas in England vor Shakespeare*, p. 10.

27. Hans Holbein, *The Dance of Death*, no. 31.

28. There are two versions of the legend. In one the living are represented as nobles; in the other, kings. These reflect the texts of two almost contemporary poems, one by Boudoin de Conde, the other by Nicholas de Marginal. See Audrey Baker, "The Interpretation and Iconography of the Longthorpe Paintings," *Archaeologia* 96 (1955): 41.

example is the beautifully illustrated Psalter of Robert de Lisle. Since we can identify the owner of the manuscript, it offers a fascinating example of an image of mortality encountered by an aristocrat in a devotional context.

The de Lisle Psalter's miniature of the Three Living and the Three Dead is a particularly fine expression of the theme. It appears as a framed diptych above the Anglo-French text of the poem. The Dead, three dark, shriveled, skeletal figures, one naked, the others dressed in ragged shrouds, stand in dramatic contrast to the three figures of the Living, crowned and finely dressed, one holding a scepter and another a falcon. Nevertheless, the relationship between the two groups is apparent in the correspondence of their gestures. The Living look with dismay on the grinning corpses, and an English inscription above the miniature sums up the confrontation in a sequence of short lines, one for each of the six figures: "Ich am afert. Lo whet Ich se. Me thinketh hit beth develes thre. Ich wes wel fair. Such scheltou be. For Godes love be wer by me." The Anglo-French text develops the Christian message:

> Ne ubliez pas pur set oysel,
> Ne pur vos robes a orfreis,
> Qe vous ne teignez bien tes leys
> Qe ihesu crist ad ordine
> De sa seinte volunte.[29]

The pleasures of courtly life distract men from the truth the corpse now understands. He exhorts the Living to turn from worldly pleasures toward the eternal ideals of Christianity. In the grave wealth and status lose all relevance:

> Ieo fu de mon lynage chief,
> Princes reys & conustables

29. Transcribed in Lucy Freeman Sandler, *The Psalter of Robert de Lisle*, p. 125 ("Do not forget for that bird or those jewelled robes that you must keep the laws that Jesus Christ ordained by his holy will").

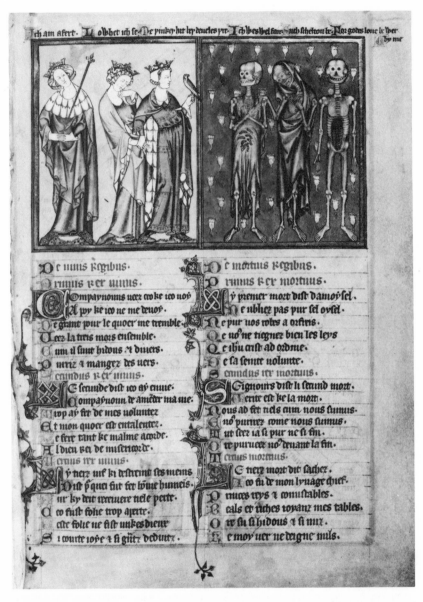

De Lisle Psalter, Miniature of the Three Living and the Three Dead. By permission of the British Library.

65

> Beals et riches ioyanz mes tables.
> Ore su si hidous & si nuz,
> Ke moy ver ne deigne nuls.[30]

Both text and illustrations contrast aristocratic life with death, insisting that the enduring fact of human existence is the reality of the grave.

Another didactic image illustrating the impermanence of courtly life is that of the Ages of Man. This popular medieval iconographic subject was illustrated in a number of ways. One of the Longthorpe Tower frescoes divides man's life into seven ages. The sequence begins with Infans, followed by Puer and Adolescens. At the apex is Vir, a lordly figure with a hawk on his left wrist. He stands full face, representing life, vigor, and mastery. Nevertheless, man's demise being as certain as his growth, Vir declines into the figure of Decrepitus, a hooded old man, supporting himself on two crutches.

Two illuminations in the Psalter of Robert de Lisle schematize human life into cycles of ten and twelve ages. These two diagrams directly precede the illumination of "The Legend of the Three Living and the Three Dead," forming a group whose purpose is to remind the reader of his mortality. Both of the diagrams of the Ages of Man are circular, each with an image of the Deity in the center and the Ages of Man in the radiating spokes of the wheel. Unlike the Longthorpe scheme, both diagrams in the Psalter of Robert de Lisle close the circle of human existence with death.

The Wheel of the Twelve Attributes of Man (fol. 126r) is divided into twelve pairs of questions and answers about birth, infancy, boyhood, adolescence, manhood, old age, decrepitude, imbecility, infirmity, dying, and death. Placed at the zenith of the circle is Vir and the question: "Tu sublimatus / In quo sis quero beatus?" ("Thou, raised aloft, in what, I ask, art thou fortunate?"). Man replies: "Viribus ornatus / In mundo vivo

---

30. Ibid., p. 125 ("I was chief of my lineage. Princes, kings and constables, fine and rich, enjoyed my tables. Now I am so hideous and so destitute that even the worms shun me").

De Lisle Psalter, The Wheel of the Ten Ages of Man. By permission of the British Library.

beatus" ("Adorned with strength, I live happy in the world"). Directly beneath Vir, at the nadir of the wheel, are Death and the question: "Dic ubi sunt gentes / ubi mundus quove parentes?" ("Say where are now the peoples, where the world, where those that gave you birth?"). The corpse replies: "Vermibus esca datus / oleo nulli modo gratus" ("Given to the worms as food, I stink, now delightful to no man"). On the other side of the folio, the Wheel of the Ten Ages of Man (fol. 126v) presents a similar scheme, although medallions containing illustrations accompany the text. In the medallion at the top of the wheel sits a crowned king holding a scepter. He says, "Rex sum rego seculum; mundus meus totus" ("I am a king. I rule the world: the whole world is mine"). The medallion at the bottom of the wheel depicts a hearse and the inscription: "Versus sum in cinerem; vita me decept" ("I am turned to ashes; life cheats me").

The de Lisle Psalter's three representations of the finiteness of courtly life prepare the aristocratic reader for receiving the devotional messages of the book as a whole. Other devotional books offer reminders of human mortality. A Psalter in the British Museum thought to have belonged to Henry IV (Cotton Domit. A.17) contains a particularly instructive illustration attached to the Office of the Dead (fol. 150v). Above a row of Cistercian monks seated in a chair stall sits a row of grinning skeletons whose crowns are the only reminder of the worldly glory they once enjoyed. Both the warrior ethic and Christian morality would agree that the manner of confronting death is central to evaluating a man's life; however, definitions of the proper response diverge so greatly that reconciliation is possible in only one circumstance — for the knight killed in the Crusades. Death in defense of the Holy Land ensures the worldly fame coveted by the warrior as well as the eternal salvation desired by the Christian. The enduring appeal of crusading owes much to its capacity for satisfying both knightly and Christian ethics. Some fourteenth-century knights engaged in Crusades in Lithuania, and some attempted to win the Holy Land for Christianity once again. For most knights, however, the attempt to synthesize the conflicting ideals of chiva-

Cotton Domit. A.17, folio 150 verso. By permission of the British Library.

lry failed, and in death they either attempted to force a compromise or chose between the heroic and Christian responses to death.

Christian and aristocratic responses to death coexist in uneasy tension in the will of the Black Prince. In the testament of one of the fourteenth century's greatest chivalric exemplars, the knight's defiance of death counters the Christian's humble acceptance. The epitaph the Black Prince chooses to adorn his tomb expresses his acceptance of death as the leveler of all men, reducing pomp and show to nothing but dust and ashes. On the other hand, his will requests a splendid funeral monument and a procession which celebrates chivalry with heraldic pageantry:

Et volons qe a quele heure qe notre corps soit amenez parmy la ville de Caterbire tantq' a la priore, q' deuz destrez covertz de noz armez et deuz homez armez en noz armez et en noz heumes voisent devant dit n're corps, c'est assavoir, l'un pur la guerre de noz armez entiers quartellez, et l'autre pur la paiz de noz bages des plumes d'ostruce ove quartre baneres de mesme la sute, et qe checun de ceux q'porteront les ditz baneres ait sur sa teste un chapeau de noz armes. Et qe celi qe fera armez pur la guerre ait un home armez portant apres li un penon de noir ove plumes d'ostruce.[31]

The Black Prince divides his identity as knight and Christian, representing the former role in heraldic symbols and the latter in his pious epitaph.

Under the strain of hostile didactic sentiment, some knights rejected the trappings of chivalry in their final testaments. The ninth Humphrey de Bohun, an active campaigner in France and Scotland, asks to be buried in the church of the Austin Friars "p' la resonn q'dieux nous ad p'stez richessez et honour en c'este

31. Nichols, ed., *A Collection of All the Wills of the Kings and Queens of England*, p. 68 ("And we wish that at that time our body be led through the town of Canterbury to the priory, that two war horses decked in our arms and two men armed in our arms and our helms attend our said body, namely, one for war in our whole arms quartered, and the other for peace in our badges of ostrich feathers with four banners of the same suit, and that each of those who carry the said banners have on his head a hat of our arms. And that he who is armed for war has an armed man carrying after him a black pennon with ostrich feathers").

seicle q'nest a la p'fyn q'ueyne gloire."[32] Richard Fitzalan, earl of Arundel and Warenne, a knight who took part in all of Edward III's important campaigns, demands, ". . . en nulle manere qe nulles genz armez, chivalx, herce, n'autre qe je n'ay devise pardevant, ne nul autre bobaunce, soient faitz entour moy."[33] Rejecting the chivalric profession at the end of their lives, these knights adopt the language of moralists.

Similarly, the will of that paragon of chivalry, Henry of Lancaster, requests a funeral without "choise voine ne de bobaunce, come les homes armeez, nedes chivals couverts, ny autres choses veines, mes une herce ove cynk cierge, chesoune cierge de centz lb, et iiii graunts mortiers, et c torches entour les corps. Et qe cynqainte poures soient vestus, vint et cynk de blank et XXV de blew, portant les ditz torches."[34] Henry's rejection of chivalric pageantry is consistent with the ambivalent tone of his *Livre de seyntz Medicines*, discussed in chapter 3. While he professes detachment from the worldly show of chivalry, his request for a procession of poor people bearing one hundred torches ensures a spectacle worthy of his rank.

Chronicles reporting fourteenth-century battles describe many instances of heroic defiance of mortality. Nonetheless, the wills of fourteenth-century knights and the antichivalric knightly productions discussed in chapter 3 demonstrate that in an unheroic context the warrior ethos fails to offer support. When passively considering their inevitable deaths, knights adopt the moralist contempt for the things of this world. The rejections of military trappings and chivalric values indicate a flaw in the fourteenth-century synthesis of chivalry. When meeting death passively, knights have to abandon their defiance and acquiesce as meekly as the humblest Christian.

32. Ibid., p. 44 ("because, in this century, God bestowed riches and honour on us, which is in the end nothing but vain glory").

33. Ibid., p. 121 (". . . in no manner shall any armed men, horses, hearse, or other thing that I did not speak of before, or any other pomp, be made about me").

34. Ibid., p. 83 (". . . vanity or pomp, such as armed men, or covered horses, or other vain things, but a hearse with five candles, each candle of a hundred pounds, and four large lamps, and a hundred torches around the body. And fifty poor people should be clothed, twenty five in white and twenty five in blue, bearing the said torches").

PART TWO

Knighthood on Trial

Chapter 5

Court and Challenger: Fitt 1

ike the open-ended conclusion of *Sir Gawain and the Green Knight*, its ambiguous opening fitt engages readers' critical faculties. While the narrative is overwhelmingly cast in the romance mode, verbal nuances suggest a competing point of view. Contrasting interpretative possibilities are most strongly represented in the figure of the Green Knight.

The opening stanzas of *Sir Gawain and the Green Knight* situate the action of the poem in the "fyrst age" of Arthur's court, evoking the continuum of Britain's mythical history reaching back to Aeneas and the founding of Rome. While the narrator warns that the nation's history alternates episodes of "boþe blysse and blunder" (line 18), readers can still anticipate a tale that will celebrate its glory, for the description of the king and his court commands superlatives (lines 51–59):

> Þe most kyd knyȝtez vnder Krystes seluen,
> And þe louelokkest ladies þat euer lif haden,
> And he þe comlokest kyng þat þe court haldes;
> For al watz þis fayre folk in her first age,
>> on sille
>> Þe hapnest vnder heuen,
>> Kyng hyȝest mon of wylle;

CONCEPTS OF CHIVALRY

Hit were now gret nye to neuen
So hardy a here on hille.

The portrait lacks any comment on the inner qualities of the court and instead praises externals: physical prowess and beauty. Since a concern with surfaces characterizes both romances and heraldic texts, readers might expect the narrative to be an uncritical celebration of aristocratic life. The "fyrst age" would then represent the mythical, golden origins of chivalry where knighthood existed in its purest form. At the same time, in recalling moralist condemnations of contemporary chivalry, this context allows equally for criticism. The poem's subtle invocation of both the courtly and the moralist perspectives colors our experience of the poem, making it difficult for us to read courtly passages without an uneasy sense of the way in which a moralist context calls romance values into question.

On the one hand, *Sir Gawain and the Green Knight* supports Derek Brewer's claim that the court represents a "splendid and admirable way of life."[1] Life at Camelot superficially reflects the fourteenth-century synthesis of courtesy, religion, and military prowess embodied in the Chandos Herald's Black Prince.[2] Arthur's knights practice their military skills in tourney and joust, observe the feast of Christmas by attending mass, and indulge in pleasant courtesies with the opposite sex. Although the element of play in their behavior suggests that chivalric obligations are taken lightly, graceful sociability is a positive quality in late medieval courtly life. At the same time the text sustains an opposite interpretation. Arthur's court celebrates the holidays "with rych reuel oryȝt and rechles merþes" (line 40). Joyous celebration is fitting (*oryȝt*) on the feast of Christ's birth, but there is a negative coloring in the adjective *rechles* with its

1. Derek Brewer, "The *Gawain* Poet: A General Appreciation of Four Poems," *EIC* 7 (1967): 136.
2. See discussion of *La vie du Prince Noir* in chap. 2. Burrow compares Arthur's gaiety to the Black Prince's. Burrow, *A Reading of* Sir Gawain and the Green Knight, p. 6.

suggestion of carelessness as well as freedom from care.[3] Leaving mass in high spirits, with "clerkez and oþer" crying "Nowel" loudly, the knights and ladies laugh merrily over what was probably a kissing game.[4] While perfectly innocent, the court's Christmas activities want seriousness. The practice of chivalry at Camelot does not seem to go beyond surface appearance.

The court's lack of sobriety leaves it open for negative interpretations. Lynn Staley Johnson brings the moralist view of chivalric accomplishments to her explication of the opening stanzas: "The poet's emphasis here upon beauty, strength, wealth, and delight suggests Camelot's vulnerability to time by describing those things that time can destroy."[5] Developing the notion of "blunder" in Britain's history, Johnson offers an interpretation of the court that is within the possibilities suggested by the text. On the other hand, she limits the poem's range of expression by interpreting its romance elements of marvel as a symptom of instability.[6] Another critic does violence to the poem by importing extraneous patristic doctrines. Judith Neaman writes, "Celebrating the New Year so riotously, Arthur is following in a long line of pagans against whose practices the church fathers, from the time of Augustine forth, felt obligated to warn all good Christians."[7] Nothing in the poem indicates that readers are to connect Camelot's celebration with such patristic admonitions. Nothing encourages critics to interpret the poem within the context of remote church history. While the opening stanzas of *Sir Gawain and the Green Knight* permit moralist readings as well as romance and heraldic ones, they do not unequivocally declare any particular perspective. To narrow the poem's opening to a single perspective is to close off the rich possibilities the text allows.

3. Ibid., pp. 7–8.
4. Oliver Farrar Emerson, "Notes on *Sir Gawain and the Green Knight*," *JEGP* 21 (1922): 365.
5. Johnson, *The Voice of the Gawain-Poet*, p. 46.
6. Ibid., p. 49.
7. Judith S. Neaman, "Sir Gawain's Covenant: Troth and *Timor Mortis*," *PQ* 55 (1976): 32.

Like the court as a whole, Arthur, its gay young king, can be judged positively or negatively, depending on the point of view adopted. In a courtly context he is attractive; to a moralist he is suspect. Burrow argues that knights are ideally jolly and gay. In the Chandos Herald's biography the Black Prince receives praise for these qualities.[8] Other adjectives would evoke the suspicion of moralists.[9] While "lyȝt" means gay or cheerful, it also intimates a lack of moral substance. "Childgered" and "wylde" suggest that the king may have lacked the maturity to govern.[10]

Unable to sit down and enjoy the feast until his youthful enthusiasm for adventure is satisfied, Arthur demands to hear a tale of "sum mayn meruayle" or to watch a joust between two knights. What he wants is a game in the heraldic or romance sense, a celebration of courtly culture in a controlled, artistic form. The entertainment Arthur calls for would be unremarkable in a fourteenth-century court,[11] yet that which appears is alien. When an "aghlich mayster" enters after the serving of the first course, the court greets his appearance with stunned silence. The narrator claims uncertainty about the meaning of their response: "I deme hit not al for doute, / Bot sum for cortaysye" (lines 246–47). In so doing, of course, he slyly suggests that Arthur's bold knights are unnerved by the appearance of the Green Knight. This tactic diminishes the distance between readers and the poem's protagonists, facilitating identification with the court, for the immense green man is as foreign to Camelot as he would be to any of Richard's royal palaces or, indeed, to twentieth-century settings. Naturalistic elements like the court's reaction encourage readers to accept as their own the problems the poem raises.

8. Burrow, *A Reading of* Sir Gawain and the Green Knight, pp. 5–6.

9. Burrow characterizes Arthur's portrait as ambivalent. Ibid., pp. 7–8.

10. Hans Schnyder, "Aspects of Kingship in 'Sir Gawain and the Green Knight,'" *ES* 40 (1959): 289–94; Johnson, *The Voice of the* Gawain *Poet*, p. 49.

11. Silverstein observes that from the fourteenth century on it was customary at English coronation feasts for the royal champion to ride in and make his challenge between the first and second courses. *Sir Gawain and the Green Knight*, ed. Silverstein, p. 119.

The introduction of the challenger underscores the necessity for readers to remain uncommitted to any single point of view, for the Green Knight does not conform to romance, heraldic, or moralist patterns for an opponent of chivalry. The challenger troubles twentieth-century critics as much as he does the court at Camelot. His ambiguity accounts for some of the poem's impenetrability, for he is unlike any stock romance antagonist. His appearance suggests opposing medieval types.[12] He has the attractiveness of a vegetation man or a courtly youth.[13] At the same time he inspires terror like the wild man or the figure of death.[14] In addition to invoking contrasting associations, the Green Knight's description unfolds in a manner that heightens his ambiguity.[15] He seems alternately terrifying and unnatural and handsome and well proportioned.

The two conflicting symbols carried by the challenger represent two possibilities for interpreting his character. The Green Knight points to the holly bob as a sign of his peaceful intent: "'Ȝe may be seker bi þis braunch þat I bere here / Þat I passe as in pes, and no plyȝt seche'" (lines 265–66). The narrator draws attention to the seasonal branch as an emblem of life and regeneration. On the other hand, the "spetos sparþe" clearly represents a mortal threat.

While the evergreen branch accords with the Green Knight's avowed intention to offer a "Crystemas gomen" rather than a battle, the ax makes the more immediate impression. Addressing the threat of violence implicit in the weapon, Arthur re-

12. Benson, *Art and Tradition*, pp. 62–95; Burrow, *A Reading of* Sir Gawain and the Green Knight, pp. 13–23.

13. Burrow, *A Reading of* Sir Gawain and the Green Knight, pp. 15–16; Benson, *Art and Tradition*, pp. 62–72; E. K. Chambers, *The Medieval Stage*, 1: 186.

14. Benson discusses his relationship to the wild man, a figure associated with winter and death. Benson, *Art and Tradition*, pp. 72–90; A. H. Krappe, "Who Was The Green Knight?" *Speculum* 13 (1938): 206–15, identifies him as the figure of death; Burrow points out echoes of "a Morality Play, a Tragedy of Princes, or an 'ubi sunt' lyric." Burrow, *A Reading of* Sir Gawain and the Green Knight, p. 26.

15. Benson discusses this technique. Benson, *Art and Tradition*, pp. 58–62; see also William Goldhurst, "The Green and the Gold: The Major Theme of *Gawain and the Green Knight*," *CE* 20 (1958): 61–65.

sponds as if he has not heard the avowals of peace and gamesmanship: "'If þou craue batayl bare, / Here faylez þou not to fyʒt'" (lines 277–78). The king's perception of the challenger's menace reflects the courtly perspective that readers are invited to adopt in the first fitt. Although the Green Knight has some attributes that indicate his nobility,[16] his game differs from the rites associated with either Camelot or fourteenth-century aristocratic culture. Taking part in the challenger's sport would entail something very different from the knightly joust Arthur envisions, where men would hazard life for life "As fortun wolde fulsun hom" (line 99). Fortune decides conventional duels, for they oppose men who are more or less social and physical equals, identically armed. Instead of chivalric combat, the Green Knight demands that some knight perform an execution and then, in turn, submit to one. For such unbalanced violence, knightly training offered no preparation. To attack an unarmed man would mean shame rather than social approval. To the court the Exchange of Winnings proposal is no game but a deadly threat.

Rather than the affirmation of courtly values Arthur had hoped for, the challenger offers a threat to Camelot's image. The Green Knight refuses the offer of battle in a manner guaranteed to stir up aggression. Scornfully he offers an estimate of the knights' prowess: "'Hit arn aboute on þis bench bot berdlez chylder. / If I were hasped in armes on a heʒe stede, / Here is no mon me to mach, for myʒtez so wayke'" (lines 280–82). The Green Knight insults the knights and then denies them the opportunity to avenge the insult in battle, a right exercised by medieval aristocrats as well as romance heroes.

The Green Knight displays much interest in the court's reputation (lines 257–64):

"To wone any quyle in þis won, hit watz not myn ernde;
Bot for þe los of þe, lede, is lyft vp so hyʒe,
And þy burʒ and þy burnes best ar holden,

---

16. Burrow, *A Reading of* Sir Gawain and the Green Knight, pp. 15–20.

Stifest vnder stel-gere on stedes to ryde,
Þe wyȝtest and þe worþyest of þe worldes kynde,
Preue for to play wyth in oþer pure laykez,
And here is kydde cortaysye, as I haf herd carp,
And þat hatz wayned me hider, iwyis, at þis tyme."

While he mentions their courtesy, the Green Knight's description of Camelot emphasizes martial accomplishments: "best," "stifest," "wyȝtest," and "worþyest." Although he applies these superlatives to the court, the challenger insists that he is repeating what others say of Arthur's knights, describing how they "ar holden" rather than how he knows them to be. He comes to test the degree to which reputation corresponds to reality: "'Bot if þou be so bold as alle burnez tellen, / Þou wyl grant me godly þe gomen þat I ask / by ryȝt'" (lines 272–73). The Green Knight's questioning of the court's reputation demands a response, for knightly honor maintains that one's name is as precious as life. Arthur's immediate rage and uncharacteristic desire to accept the challenge himself attests the seriousness of the affront.

The Green Knight's final words to Gawain at Camelot reiterate his concern with reputation: "'Þerfore com, oþer recreaunt be calde þe behoues'" (line 456). The epithet "recreaunt" commonly applies to knights who have abused the tenets of chivalry and earned dishonor. While I do not agree with Benson's claim that renown is the central theme of the poem,[17] knightly concern with reputation plays a critical role. Renown is part of the broader theme of chivalric conduct.[18] The poem's hero must, like historical knights of the fourteenth century, authenticate his ideals through action.

Although the Green Knight's challenge qualifies as a romance marvel, his portrayal does not conform to that of a conventional romance challenger. His presence suggests a moralist reproach to

17. Benson, *Art and Tradition*, p. 209.
18. I agree with Everett that the poem's first concern is with conduct, although I take it to be knightly conduct in particular. Everett, *Essays on Middle English Literature*, p. 77.

chivalry. The silence greeting the Green Knight's invitation to the game underscores its alien and distasteful nature. The scene is reminiscent of the moment in the fifteenth-century English poem of the Three Living and the Three Dead when the turbulence of the hunt is silenced by the entrance of the Three Dead.[19] When the court fails to respond to his invitation, the Green Knight mockingly insinuates that their high reputation is unfounded (lines 309–15):

> "What, is þis Arþures hous," quoþ þe haþel þenne,
> "þat al þe rous rennes of þurȝ ryalmes so mony?
> Where is now your sourquydrye and your conquestes,
> Your gryndellayk and your greme, and your grete wordes?
> Now is þe reuel and þe renoun of þe Rounde Table
> Overwalt wyth a worde of on wyȝes speche,
> For al dares for drede withoute dynt schewed!"

The echo of the ubi sunt formula in lines 311–12 reinforces the association of the Green Knight with death.[20] The challenger silences the court and overwhelms their worldly attainments just as the corpses do in "The Legend of the Three Living and the Three Dead."

Readers can adopt the moralist perspective and understand the challenger as a reminder of man's inevitable end in time.[21] Conversely, they may respond as Camelot seems to and interpret the Green Knight's presence as an unchivalric intrusion into a courtly setting.[22] Aspects of his portrait resemble the churlish characters who serve as foils to the heroes of a number of romances.[23]

The duality in the Green Knight's gestures of peace and

19. John Audelay, *The Poems of John Audelay*, ed. Ella K. Whiting, EETS o.s., vol. 184 (1930), no. 54, pp. 217–23; cited in Phillipa Tristram, *Figures of Life and Death in Medieval English Literature*, pp. 164–65.
20. Burrow, *A Reading of* Sir Gawain and the Green Knight, p. 26.
21. Howard, *The Three Temptations*, pp. 230–32.
22. John Speirs, *Medieval English Poetry: The Non-Chaucerian Tradition*, p. 226.
23. Benson, *Art and Tradition*, pp. 83–90.

aggression and his symbols of life and death corresponds to representations of mortality in medieval art and literature. For the well-prepared Christian death signifies peace and new life; for the unprepared soul it is cause for terror. For the warrior who falls in battle, death brings the consolation of fame and glory; for the knight who must face his end passively, chivalric courage is likely to falter.

Gawain's request for the game represents an attempt to restore the court's reputation in the face of the challenge. He requests the contest briefly: "'I beseche now with saȝes sene / Þis melly mot be myne'" (lines 341–42), but he continues his speech at some length, offering a consummate display of tact and courtliness. With great deference to Guinevere he asks Arthur to allow him to leave the table. He then insists on the propriety of one of Arthur's knights taking up the challenge in place of the King, a point consistent with the tenets of feudal chivalry. Finally, with exaggerated humility, Gawain insists on his own unworthiness, meekly attributing any virtue he might have to his kinship with Arthur.

Gawain's display of knightly manners is all the more impressive when contrasted with the response of the rest of the court. While the others are struck dumb with fear, Gawain regains enough composure to represent Arthur very creditably against the stranger's challenge. He soothes the affront to Camelot's reputation by contrasting himself with the King and court (lines 351–55):

> "...mony so bold yow aboute vpon bench sytten,
> Þat vnder heuen I hope no haȝerer of wylle,
> Ne better bodyes on bent þer baret is rered.
> I am þe wakkest, I wot, and of wyt feblest,
> And lest lur of my lyf, quo laytes þe soþe — "

Gawain's humility consists of an extravagant display of politeness in the chivalric mode. Although ostensibly complimenting Camelot's knights, the hero's self-abasement draws attention to his own courtly accomplishments. He applies comparative terms to the knights, "non haȝerer" and "no better," and superlatives to himself, "wakkest," "feblest," and "lest." At the same time he acknowledges the mortal implication of the Green Knight's challenge in observing that Arthur's knights are better suited for battle and by claiming that his life would be missed least.

The beheading itself differs notably from most other romance combats. The challenger submits passively to Gawain's blow, bowing his head to expose "the naked nec" (line 420). Chivalric prowess plays no part in the contest. The weight of the ax does the work as Gawain lets the blade down easily on the challenger's neck so that "þe scharp of þe schalk schyndered þe bones, / And schrank þurȝ þe schyire grece, and schade hit in twynne" (lines 424–25). The spectators respond not with admiration but with apparent distaste, kicking the severed head as it rolls on the ground.

The ending of the first fitt affords contradictory readings. Images of mortality strongly suggest a moralist interpretation. When the Green Knight brandishes his head above his grotesquely bleeding body, the implications of the figure of Death in his portrait emerge more strongly. Death is, after all, the only deathless warrior. The severed head, reminding Gawain of his appointment on New Year's morning, suggests moralist memento mori images. A moralist reading of the first fitt would represent the challenger as a reproach to Camelot, condemning the court for its worldliness. Reinforcing this impression, the narrator's comment punctuating the first fitt sounds a somewhat cautionary note (lines 487–90):

> Now þenk wel, Sir Gawan,
> For woþe þat þou ne wonde
> Þis auenture for to frayn
> Þat þou hatz tan on honde.

Nonetheless, the admonition to the hero contains no censure. It could even serve to enhance readers' impressions of Gawain when, in the second fitt, he sets out on his perilous quest.

Readers favoring a courtly interpretation of Camelot might note that the first fitt ends with the romance atmosphere of the opening stanzas restored. The feast continues "Wyth alle maner of mete and mynstralcie boþe / Wyth wele walt þay þat day" (lines 484–85). Though the Green Knight's presence has disturbed Camelot's contained world, courtly gaiety returns to the holiday celebration. With admirable control Arthur hides his concern, assuring the Queen "wyth cortays speche" that what she has seen is a fitting entertainment for Christmas (lines 470–73). As a reminder of the marvel which has occurred, the Green Knight's huge ax hangs above the dais, to be interpreted either as a symbol of the court's triumph over the otherworldly challenger or as a sign of the inescapable fact of human mortality invoked by moralists to demonstrate worldly vanity.

Chapter 6

The Pentangle Knight, Alone and in Hall:
Fitt 2

t Camelot, in the first fitt of *Sir Gawain and the Green
Knight*, chivalry appears as a social code defining the
aristocracy. When Gawain requests the Green Knight's
challenge, he does so as Arthur's nephew, a representative of the court. His actions restore a semblance of the gaiety
and confidence which characterizes the court at the start of the
poem. The second fitt presents both a change of mood and a new
view of the hero. Gawain becomes isolated, separated by the
personal version of chivalry defined in his pentangle and by the
attitude of both the court and the narrator. On his journey the
hero is no longer the familiar "gode Gawan." Instead, alone and
at Bertilak's court, he must define himself continuously by his
actions.

At the beginning of the second fitt the narrator becomes
moralistic in speaking of Gawain's forthcoming adventure. Replacing the approving tone of the first fitt is detached censure
(lines 495–99):

Gawan watz glad to begynne þose gomnez in halle,
Bot þaȝ þe ende be heuy haf ȝe no wonder;
For þaȝ men ben mery in mynde quen þay han mayn drynk,

87

A ȝere ȝernes ful ȝerne, and ȝeldez neuer lyke,
Þe forme to þe fynisment foldez ful selden.

For the first time the moralist perspective is explicitly invoked.
While these sentiments may prepare us for the more somber tone
of the second fitt, the disjunction between the elapsed action and
the narrator's censure calls into question narrowly moralistic
interpretations. Scattergood accepts this passage as an index of
the hero's moral weakness,[1] but attributing Gawain's courageous
and dangerous undertaking to the influence of strong drink
seems unjust. To begin with, the Green Knight issues his challenge before the New Year's feast is fully under way. Second, the
hero's careful speech betrays no evidence of his inebriation.
Rather than applying specifically to Gawain's situation, the passage echoes moral aphorisms and recalls the view of man's decline
in time in the tradition of Seneca and the Christian homilists.[2]
Just as certain elements of the first fitt prompt readers to question
the courtly mode, here the discrepancy between the action and
the narrator's commentary prevents us from accepting narrowly
moralistic interpretations uncritically. Nevertheless, the narrator's comment serves to isolate the hero and to heighten the
sense of impending doom.

The narrator's subsequent evocation of the passing of the
seasons functions similarly, but in a more lyrical fashion. Rather
than emphasizing spring and nature's renewal (a more common
topos in romance), the passage insists on the return of winter and
the inevitability of death (lines 527–31):

And al grayes þe gres þat grene watz ere;
Þenne al rypez and rotez þat ros vpon fyrst,
And þus ȝirnez þe ȝere in ȝisterdayez mony,

---

1. Scattergood, "Literary Culture at the Court of Richard II," pp. 252–55.
2. See Silverstein's Introduction to *Sir Gawain and the Green Knight*, p. 7, and
notes to lines 496–99; also Theodore Silverstein, "The Art of Sir Gawain and the Green
Knight," *UTQ* 33 (1964): 259ff.

THE PENTANGLE KNIGHT

And wynter wyndez aȝayn, as þe worlde askez,
no fage,

Here the poem offers the moralist's view of human life, emphasizing decline and death as the consummation of human existence — the point where the wheel of life inevitably comes to rest
for the individual. The expectations that this passage occasions
conflict with those prompted by the narrator's celebration of the
court in the opening stanzas. Larry Benson remarks the contrast
in tone between the romance and moralist passages, explaining it
as a move from fiction "into the context of the real world."[3] In
fact, romance and moralist passages should be viewed equally as
literary constructs. Just as winter and spring represent alternating
seasons in an annual cycle, so courtly and moralist views account
for different facets of human experience. *Sir Gawain and the
Green Knight* does not insist that readers attach more weight to
one perspective than the other.

Interestingly, Arthur's court abandons their courtly perspective
for an alternative, but no more convincing, interpretation of
Gawain's situation. At first the court attempts to maintain a
carefree pose while celebrating All Hallow's Day: "Mony ioylez
for þat ientyle iapez þer maden" (line 542). Camelot's characteristic gaiety is strained by the nature of Gawain's encounter with
the Green Knight. Since there seems to be no hope that the hero's
prowess will save him, the court mourns him as if they will never
see him again. To the other knights the adventure is inappropri-
ate for the hero, for it involves simply enduring a blow rather than
actively responding. Once Gawain has left, they voice their
despondency as anger. They see no glory in Gawain's adventure,
only folly (lines 674–83):

> . . . "Bi Kryst, hit is scaþe
> Þat þou, leude, schal be lost, þat art of lyf noble!
> To fynde hys fere vpon folde, in fayth, is not eþe.

3. Benson, *Art and Tradition*, p. 204.

> Warloker to haf wroȝt had more wyt bene,
> And haf dyȝt ȝonder dere a duk to have worþed;
> A lowande leder of ledez in londe hym wel semez,
> And so had better haf ben þen britned to noȝt,
> Hadet wyth an aluisch mon, for angardez pryde.
> Who knew euer any kyng such counsel to take
> As knyȝtez in cauelaciounz on Crystmasse gomnez!"

The court sees the passive death anticipated for Gawain as a waste, an event with no redeeming value. Since they see no glory in his adventure, they deny him any praise for his courage in either accepting the challenge or keeping his word to the Green Knight. Ignoring Gawain's concern with Camelot's reputation, they abandon the usual aristocratic perspective and speak of the "wyt" of proceeding more carefully and of the hero's "angardez pryde." They deny the values both of the romance, in which a challenge is taken up unhesitatingly, and of fourteenth-century heraldic texts, in which honor and reputation are paramount. Camelot's sudden practicality compares with the unchivalric viewpoint expressed later by the servant from Bertilak's court who conducts Gawain to the green chapel.[4]

In criticizing the hero's quest, the court disrupts convention. The hero of this poem does not ride out, as most Arthurian knights do, with the support of his peers. The hero's adventure cuts him off from the court in more than just a physical sense, for Arthur's knights disassociate themselves from a quest wherein they see neither glory nor hope of return. Camelot's departure from romance norms prompts readers to evaluate the action. Gawain's knightly integrity appears more attractive than the court's uncharacteristic caution. Without their support Gawain attempts to keep his agreement with the Green Knight out of a personal commitment to romance and heraldic values.

Gawain's isolation at the start of his quest, suggested by the

---

4. In suggesting that Gawain abandon his quest and promising to keep his flight secret, the guide acts as a foil to the hero, reminding the reader of the pragmatic attitude adopted by ordinary people.

attitudes of the court and the narrator, becomes formalized in the *topos* of the hero arming.[5] Through the ritual of arming, Gawain becomes not only a representative of chivalry but also an individual whose actions substantiate his own definition of himself. Part of the description of Gawain's dress characterizes him as a member of the military and courtly elite. In addition to his armor—a costly version of the type fashionable in the late fourteenth century—Gawain wears a fine embroidered silk band on his helmet, so richly decorated that the narrator surmises "As mony burde þeraboute had ben seuen wynter in toune" (lines 613–14). These accouterments demonstrate Gawain's noble status as much as his speech, his kinship with Arthur, and his comrades, "þe best of þe burʒ" (line 550). The final item of Gawain's armor, his shield, is distinctive. Its emblem is unique to this poem and should be taken as a personal symbol, crucial to readers' understanding of Gawain's character and helpful in explaining his subsequent behavior.

The narrator indicates the importance of the pentangle "þat bisemed þe segge semlyly fayre" (line 622) by pointing out that he will describe "quy þe pentangel apendez to þat prynce noble / . . . þof tary hyt me schulde" (lines 623–24). In describing Gawain's pentangle, the narrator suggests that the symbol represents the hero's reputation (lines 631–39):

> Forþy hit acordez to þis knyʒt and to his cler armez,
> For ay faythful in fyue and sere fyue syþez
> Gawan watz for gode knawen, and as gold pured,
> Voyded of vche vylany, wyth vertuez ennourned
> in mote;
> Forþy þe pentangel nwe
> He ber in schelde and cote,
> As tulk of tale most trwe
> And gentylest knyʒt of lote.

5. Derek Brewer, "The Arming of the Warrior in European Literature and Chaucer," in Edward Vasta and Zacharias P. Thundy, eds., *Chaucerian Problems and Perspectives*, pp. 221–43; Burrow, *A Reading of* Sir Gawain and the Green Knight, pp. 37–38.

CONCEPTS OF CHIVALRY

The constellation of virtues the pentangle represents are those for which the hero "watz for gode knawen." He bears the sign as a man true of "tale," an ambiguous phrase which suggests both that he is true of speech and also that he conforms to report, or reputation. The hero's words and promises about himself are critical to his identity, as are the words spoken by others about him. As heraldic custom dictates, the hero's actions must conform to the image that his shield presents to the world.

Gawain's pentangle demonstrates that the chivalric ethos practiced so lightly at court is of the highest seriousness to the poem's hero. For Gawain, the military, religious, and courtly elements of chivalry observed in social rituals at Camelot carry significance as personal ideals.[6] While his military prowess is mentioned, "fayled neuer þe freke in his fyue fyngres" (line 641),[7] most strongly emphasized is the knight's piety, indicated by his faith in the five wounds and his devotion to the five joys of "þe hende heuen-quene" (line 647) whose image is painted on the inside of his shield. The courtly aspects of chivalry appear in the "fifth five" Gawain practices: "fraunchyse and felaȝschyp forbe al þyng, / His clannes and his cortaysye croked were neuer, / And pité, þat passez alle poyntez" (lines 652–54). These abstract virtues recall the idealistic chivalric literature read during the fourteenth century, like Lull's *Le Libre del Orde de Cavalleria*. They indicate Gawain's self-consciousness about his vocation and distinguish him from his peers at Camelot.

The pentangle is an apt symbol of the tension which holds together Gawain's idealistic form of chivalry. The knight's virtues should cohere just as the five points of the pentangle unite into a single figure (lines 657–60):

> And vchone halched in oþer, þat non ende hade,
> And fyched vpon fyue poyntez, þat fayld neuer,

6. Engelhardt divides Gawain's virtues into a similar grouping of valor, piety, and courtesy. George J. Engelhardt, "The Predicament of Gawain," *MLQ* 16 (1955): 219.

7. A literal interpretation seems more satisfactory than the penitential reading of this line offered by Robert W. Ackerman, "Gawain's Shield: Penitential Doctrine in *Sir Gawain and the Green Knight*," *Anglia* 76 (1958): 254–65.

Ne samned neuer in no syde, ne sundred nouþer,
Withouten ende at any noke I oquere fynde.

The symbol implies that the true pentangle knight, the exemplar
of chivalry, will maintain all his virtues without a lapse, for any
break in the symbol would alter its nature. Nevertheless, the
synthesis of chivalric qualities is tenuous, for the pentangle signifies a threefold commitment to God, the King, and ladies. The
tension implicit in this tripartite allegiance is somewhat reconciled by the inclusion of "clannes," among the hero's chivalric
attributes. Where the Black Prince of the Chandos Herald's
portrait reconciled his allegiance to God and women in a Christian marriage to Joan of Kent, Gawain embraces both chastity
and courtesy. Gawain's rejection of adultery, almost a require-
ment of courtliness in some romances,[8] negates the threat that an
adulterous relationship posed to religious and feudal chivalry.
Gawain's "clannes" alerts the reader that he is not the libidinous
Gawain of French romance tradition but the more virtuous character of English romance.[9] In juxtaposing "clannes" and "cortaysye," the description draws attention to the uncompromising
nature of Gawain's idealism. Moreover, the pentangle passage
prepares readers for a test that involves more than a trial of
courage. A multifaceted adventure can be anticipated for the
knight whose definition of chivalry unites disparate virtues into a
single emblem.

The narrator sharpens the sense of Gawain's separation from
the court by plotting a journey that would have signified a
departure from civilized society for the poem's original audience.
After riding through the mythical realm of Logres, Gawain
crosses terrain that was notoriously untamed in the fourteenth
century—"þe wyldreness of Wyrale; wonde þer bot lyte / Þat

8. C. S. Lewis makes Adultery one of the four characteristics of courtly love. Lewis,
The Allegory of Love, p. 12.
9. Benson, *Art and Tradition*, pp. 95–96; B. J. Whiting, "Gawain: His Reputation,
His Courtesy and His Appearance in Chaucer's *Squire's Tale*," *MS* 9 (1947): 189–234.

auþer God oþer gome wyth goud hert louied" (lines 701–702).[10] Gawain's quest brings him to parts remote from familiar companions and from a society that would honor chivalric values.

On his journey Gawain encounters the kinds of adversaries common in romance: dragons, wolves, wood men, bulls, bears, boars, and giants. Nonetheless, the narrator shows little interest in this type of adventure: "Hit were to tore for to telle of þe tenþe dole" (line 719). Gawain easily dispatches this kind of challenge; what troubles him instead is the timeless human battle against the elements (lines 726–30):

> For werre wrathed hym not so much þat wynter nas wors,
> When þe colde cler water fro þe cloudez schadde,
> And fres er hit falle myȝt to þe fale erþe;
> Ner slayn wyth þe slete he sleped in his yrnes
> Mo nyȝtez þen innoghe in naked rokkez.

The narrator focuses on a scene alien to both romance and to heraldic reports of battles and deeds of arms, yet common to human experience.[11] Perhaps more than anything else, Gawain's predicament recalls Geoffroi de Charny's frank accounts of the discomforts of campaigning. The image of Gawain huddled among inhospitable rocks in the inclement weather emphasizes the hero's mortality. While his armor offers protection in battle, it affords him no ease in the winter sleet. The poet's choice of the word "yrnes" instead of "armes" or "harnays" draws attention to the uncomfortable metallic war gear and underscores the hero's distress. This passage anticipates Gawain's predicament in meeting the Green Knight and exposing his unprotected neck to the sharp metal blade of the ax.

---

10. See H. L. Savage, "A Note on Gawain and the Green Knight (700–2)," *MLN* 46 (1931): 455–57.

11. See Derek Pearsall and Elizabeth Salter, *Landscapes and Seasons of the Medieval World*, pp. 148–53. The authors find that the poet departs from the landscape conventions of poetry and painting and substantiates "the quality of winter in a series of startling and evocative natural images" (p. 148).

Weary of battling the elements alone, Gawain prays for "sum herber" (line 755). Yet he does not seek refuge solely to protect himself from the harsh outdoors. He is also concerned with acting as a Christian knight should on Christmas Eve: "Carande for his costes lest he ne keuer schulde / To se þe seruyse of þat syre þat on þat self nyȝt / Of a burde watz borne oure baret to quelle" (lines 750–53). That Gawain should be seen as feeling a spiritual as well as a physical compulsion is confirmed by his penitential mood, as he cries for his misdeeds and crosses himself. The immediate appearance of a castle in the wilderness is a phenomenon acceptable through those romance conventions which remove the necessity for logical justification. The castle materializes in response to Gawain's desire; hence its appearance does not immediately seem connected to the hero's test. Only later does it become apparent that, rather than offering an interlude of rest, the castle provides the setting for more trials.

Bertilak's court seems so like Arthur's that it appears to offer Gawain a familiar refuge in alien territory.[12] The orderliness and beauty of the castle recall the civilized world of Arthur's court, and, like Camelot, Hautdesert evokes superlative terms: "A castel þe comlokest þat euer knyzt aȝte" (line 767) and "A better barbican þat burne blusched vpon neuer" (line 793). Gawain is welcomed as warmly as if he had arrived at Camelot. First the porter assures him "'purely I trowee / Þat ȝe be, wyȝe, welcum to won quyle yow lykez'" (lines 813–14). Next the host assures him that "'al is yowre awen, to haue at yowre wylle and welde'" (lines 836–37). Of course, these greetings anticipate the abundant hospitality offered by the lady in her seduction attempt: "Ȝe ar welcum to my cors, / Yowre awen won to wale" (lines 1237–38).

---

12. Burrow points out some parallels between the two courts to show a correspondence between the Beheading and the Exchange of Winnings games. Burrow, *A Reading of* Sir Gawain and the Green Knight, pp. 65–66; Brewer notes the similarities, though he sees them as an artistic flaw, since "the court of Bertilak is deeply hostile to Arthur and Gawain." Brewer, "The Gawain Poet," p. 136. Other readers point out differences: Scattergood, for example, characterizes Bertilak's court as more provincial than Arthur's. Scattergood, "Literary Culture at the Court of Richard II," p. 252.

The congeniality of the host and servants puts Gawain at ease. Exchanging his armor for rich robes and a warm, fur-lined mantle, he seems far safer than he had been battling the cold on his journey.

The household's reception of the news of Gawain's identity introduces a new perspective on the hero. First the narrator summarizes Gawain's reputation: "Þat alle prys and prowes and pured þewes / Apendes to hys persoun, and praysed is euer; / Byfore alle men vpon molde his mensk is þe most" (lines 912–14). This brief evaluation vaguely echoes the narrator's extended description in the pentangle passage. The "pured þewes" recall the comparison to "golde pured" (line 633), and the only other appearance of the verb "apende" is in line 623: "And quy þe pentangel apendez to þat prince noble." While this description of Gawain's virtues is less detailed and less specific than the pentangle passage, its general terms convey a sense of the knight's multifaceted accomplishment. The "prys" and "prowes" denote his martial excellence, while the "pured þewes" could embrace both his "clannes" and his "cortaysye." By contrast, Bertilak's household defines the guest's attributes more narrowly in terms of the social graces belonging to knights (lines 916–27):

> "Now schal we semlych se sleȝtez of þewez
> And þe teccheles termes of talkyng noble,
> Wich spede is in speche vnspurd may we lerne,
> Syn we haf fonged þat fyne fader of nurture.
> God hatz geuen vus his grace godly for soþe,
> Þat such a gest as Gawan grauntez vus to haue,
> When burnez blyþe of his burþe schal sitte
> and synge.
> In menyng of manerez mere
> Þis burne now schal vus bryng,
> I hope þat may hym here,
> Schal lerne of luf-talkyng."

Bertilak's court translates Gawain's high virtues into the social attributes of refined manners and noble speech. Finally, in the rhyming quatrain (the wheel) that completes the stanza, the hero's chivalry is reduced to a single accomplishment: "luf-talkyng." Gawain's hosts demand not the complex ethical chivalry defined in the pentangle but rather a display of social skills that conforms to the practice at Camelot. If the hero abides by a more idealistic version of knighthood, his personal ethos guides him rather than the expectations of others.

At Hautdesert the only suggestion of the theme of mortality is expressed indirectly in the contrast between Lady de Hautdesert and her companion, the "auncian" who is later identified as Morgan la Faye. The appealing features of Bertilak's young wife have their negative counterpart in the appearance of her shriveled companion (lines 951–63):

> For if þe ȝonge watz ȝep, ȝolȝe watz þat oþer;
> Riche red on þat on rayled ayquere,
> Rugh ronkled chekez þat oþer on rolled;
> Kerchofes of þat on, wyth mony cler perlez,
> Hir brest and hir bryȝt þrote bare displayed,
> Schon schyrer þen snawe þat schedez on hillez;
> Þat oþer wyth a gorger watz gered ouer þe swyre,
> Chymbled ouer hir blake chyn with chalkquyte vayles,
> Hir frount folden in sylk, enfoubled ayquere,
> Toreted and treleted with tryflez aboute,
> Þat noȝt watz bare of þat burde bot þe blake broȝes,
> Þe tweyne yȝen and þe nase, þe naked lyppez,
> And þose were soure to se and sellyly blered.

The language of the young woman's portrait evokes images of life, while the old woman's description conjures up decay. The first face is fresh and rosy like a ripe apple, while the second is withered and wrinkled like fruit kept too long. While the young woman's bare skin, abundantly displayed, shines with the newness of snow, the older woman covers her darkened skin with veils the color of chalk, an image which suggests a shrouded corpse. Presenting a mute version of the moralist perspective on aristocratic life, the contrast between their two portraits suggests both the two female figures of Life and Death in the alliterative poem *Death and Liffe* and the complementary images of the Three Living and the Three Dead.[13]

Although the description of the two women recalls didactic comparisons, the narrator ostensibly presents them from the aristocratic point of view. Though the younger lady displays an expanse of flesh, the narrator makes the older seem more obscene, with her "naked lyppez / . . .soure to se." The narrator concedes the possibility of a different perspective wherein age is worthy of respect: "A mensk lady on molde mon may hir calle, / for Gode!" (lines 964–65). Nevertheless, he concludes the portrait by returning to physical rather than moral distinctions (lines 966–69):

> Hir body watz schort and þik,
> Hir buttokez balʒ and brode,
> Mor lykkerwys on to lyk
> Watz þat scho hade on lode.

The adjective *lykkerwys*, connoting something sweet to eat as well as to look at, continues the association with fresh fruit, drawing attention to the younger woman's sensuous appeal.

Not perceiving the reminder of earthly transience embodied in the juxtaposition of the two women, Gawain views his stay in the castle as an interlude between considerations of mortality. Evaluating the two from a courtly perspective, Gawain bows to the older while "Þe loueloker he lappez a lyttel in armez, / He kysses hir comlyly" (lines 973–74). More than anything else the castle has to offer, the lady promises to dispel Gawain's thoughts of mortality with those of life, and it is in her company that Gawain takes great delight during the days of feasting over Christmas.

13. *Death and Liffe*, ed. Israel Gollancz, in *Select Early English Poems*. For an example of the mirroring of the Three Living and the Three Dead, see the de Lisle Psalter, described in chap. 3, where the attitudes of the dead in the main miniature reflect those of the living and where the text underscores the connection: "Ich wes wel fair. Such scheltou be. For Godes love be wer by me."

With Gawain readers are unaware of the host's identity and purpose during the time Gawain spends at the castle. Though there are subtle echoes of the Green Knight in Bertilak's portrait, nothing indicates that the host has met Gawain previously. In fact, the narrator describes how the castle's inhabitants gradually learn of Gawain's identity "bi preué poyntez" (line 902). On learning that the guest is Gawain, Bertilak and his household respond with delight and apparent surprise. Having no more idea than Gawain of the intimate connection between his stay at the castle and his assignation at the green chapel, readers must initially allow the plot to unfold before interpreting the moralist imagery of the women's portraits.

In retrospect the household at Hautdesert can be seen as deliberately conspiring to lower the hero's guard, but a first-time reader sees this no better than does Gawain. The narrative's elements of mystery thus align readers with the hero. Hautdesert seems to represent nothing more than a setting in which Gawain can display his social graces. On a first reading of the poem, Bertilak's proposal for the Exchange of Winnings seems an inconsequential game rather than a test. The host's apparently spontaneous suggestions do not indicate a premeditated plot. First, Bertilak makes Gawain promise to do as he commands, a proposal which only makes explicit the allegiance Gawain already owes in accepting the lord's hospitality. Then he tells Gawain to linger in his room resting on the next morning and to enjoy his wife's company for the day while he rises early to hunt. Finally, the host casually proposes that they contract to exchange the winnings of the next day. After sealing the bargain with drink and exchanging compliments and kisses, they go to bed. The narrator concludes the episode with the apparently innocent observation: "Þe olde lorde of þat leude / Cowþe wel halde layk alofte" (lines 1124–25), eliciting the expectation that Bertilak will merely entertain his guest by continuing to extend him hospitality and by indulging in a harmless game with him.

Ironically, Gawain's participation in a situation in which he can be tempted is a function of his vocation as a knight. Courtesy ensures that he will accept the host's suggestions so as not to offend. Similarly, courtesy makes unthinkable a direct rebuff of the hostess's advances. Through knightly graciousness Gawain places himself in a position where the uninterrupted harmony of the loyalties delineated in the pentangle is threatened, for the temptation strains his allegiance to Bertilak, to the hostess, and to his own pentangle ideals. *Sir Gawain and the Green Knight* depicts a situation which dramatizes the tension arising from the competing demands of the fourteenth-century synthesis of military, religious, and courtly chivalry.

Chapter 7

Indoor and Outdoor Games: Fitt 3

tructured by the three days of the Exchange of Winnings game, the third fitt of *Sir Gawain and the Green Knight* is an interlace of contrasting courtly games.[1] The hunt and the bedroom scenes are similar in that they enact rituals demonstrating the nobility's mastery of primal impulses.[2] In fact, the narrator characterizes both as games.[3] In the context of controlled aristocratic play, the hero's instinctual fear of death rises to the surface, leading to his violation of chivalric rules.

As Bertilak's entourage prepares for the hunt at the start of the third fitt, the poem conveys a sense of vitality even though the purpose of the ritual is the death of the quarry. Full of very concrete verbs, the first stanza depicts a scene of purposeful

---

1. Some critics have attempted to draw elaborate parallels between the hunt and the bedroom scenes; see in particular Savage, "The Significance of the Hunting Scenes," pp. 1–15; Gerald Gallant, "The Three Beasts: Symbols of Temptation in *Sir Gawain and the Green Knight*," *AnM* 11 (1970): 35–50; W. R. J. Barron, *Trawþe and Treason*. My own interpretation follows Burrow's suggestion (p. 87) that the third fitt develops the contrast between indoor and outdoor experience.

2. See Charles Muscatine, *Poetry and Crisis in the Age of Chaucer*, pp. 61–67, and my discussion of game in romance, chap. 2.

3. Martin Stevens, "Laughter and Game in *Sir Gawain and the Green Knight*," *Speculum* 47 (1972): 72.

activity in the early-morning preparations. The chase itself continues the impression of motion and adds to it sound—the baying of hounds, the calling of the hinds, the driving of the does "with gret dyn" (line 1159), the crying of wounded deer, and the noise of the hunters' horns sounding "Wyth such a crakkande kry as klyffes haden brusten" (line 1166). The commotion should not be seen as chaotic, for the huntsmen follow prescribed rules.[4] They do not kill randomly but spare male deer, which are out of season. The noisy shouts and blasts of the horn are part of the ritual set out in manuals of the hunt. The elaborate game of hunting celebrates life and the chivalric triumph over death. The ritual particularly indicates the host's prowess as he "drof þat day wyth joy / Thus to the derk nyȝt" (lines 1176–77). The choice of the verb *drof* emphasizes the lord's mastery, making him seem as powerful as Phoebus, taking control of the forces of light and dark.

By contrast, Gawain lies passively in bed, "cortyned aboute" (line 1181), protected from the natural world outside. Nonetheless, like the hunt, the bedroom scene offers a version of the chase. It too consists of a display of peculiarly aristocratic behavior as Gawain attempts to assert his control of sexual impulses through the rituals of courtly manners.[5]

Although the narrator offers no moral commentary on the juxtaposed activities, interpreters have felt obliged to pass judgment. Silverstein argues that Gawain's inactivity leaves him open to temptation, while the host exercises virtue in hunting. Accusing Gawain of idleness, Thiebaux and Silverstein point to the lessons offered by preachers about the dangers of sloth leading to

4. Savage, *The* Gawain-*Poet*, p. 36; Stevens, "Laughter and Game in *Sir Gawain and the Green Knight*," p. 73.

5. Taking Andreas Capellanus as the authority on courtly love, Stevens argues that Gawain and the hostess violate the rules of behavior for the bedroom game. Stevens, "Laughter and Game in *Sir Gawain and the Green Knight*, pp. 74–75. I would argue that the guidelines for courtly exchanges between the sexes are far less rigidly defined that those for hunting.

lechery.[6] In viewing the chase as virtuous, these critics follow a justification offered in aristocratic hunting manuals.[7] Although such manuals appropriate the language of homilectic attacks on sloth, the poem does not echo them. In *Sir Gawain and the Green Knight* the hunt is morally neutral; it represents a violent, noisy, colorful celebration of life. Nothing in the narrative suggests that Bertilak is to be seen as more virtuous than Gawain in his choice of activity. After Gawain has spent almost two months on horseback, to accuse him of sloth seems excessive.[8] Although we have already seen that the narrator occasionally adopts the moralist voice, the descriptions of the hunt and of Gawain's indoor recreation are generally in the romance mode and contain no explicit judgment of the participants. The arguments for Gawain's sins of the flesh depend largely on citing the works of medieval moralists rather than accounting for how the text suggests that readers interpret it.

Nonetheless, scenes of the hunt and the bedroom stand clearly in contrast. Outside, Bertilak's noble pursuits are physical and unambiguous. Inside, Gawain must proceed very cautiously so as neither to compromise the ethos represented by his pentangle nor to offend his host and the social values of the Round Table. Where the hunt seems to involve no moral issues, the bedroom scenes provide the focus for some of the tensions in the different versions of fourteenth-century chivalry that the poem invokes.

The contrast between the two aristocratic pastimes is immediately apparent in the hero's confusion as the host's wife steals upon him. While Bertilak's hunt demands direct action, Gawain responds to the lady's entry with the subterfuge of feigning sleep.

6. Marcelle Thiebaux, *The Stag of Love*, p. 76; she cites *The Parson's Tale* and *The Tale of Melibee*. Silverstein (*Sir Gawain and the Green Knight*) cites the *Ayenbite of Inwyt*, pp. 47–48; *The Book of Vices and Virtues*, pp. 26–27; and *Jacob's Well*, p. 104. See notes to lines 1178ff.

7. *Sir Gawain and the Green Knight*, ed. Silverstein, p. 10; Thiebaux, *The Stag of Love*, pp. 75–80.

8. Perhaps the most elaborate argument for Gawain's sloth is Scattergood's ("Literary Culture at the Court of Richard II").

Then, concerned with the possible outcome of the situation, he adopts a new tactic: "'More semly hit were / To aspye wyth my spelle in space quat ho wolde'" (lines 1198–99). Clearly Gawain is concerned with social propriety, seemliness. His reputation for courtliness makes it unthinkable that he rebuff his hostess directly. Although the poem has previously illustrated the hero's considerable savoir faire, the ambiguity of the situation disturbs his composure.

Although the chamber could be a rather public place in the Middle Ages, with formal meetings being conducted from the bed, the lady's secretive entrance clearly represents a possibly compromising situation. Gawain's act of crossing himself alerts readers to the potential danger. The lady acknowledges the threat implicit in her presence in her first words: "Ȝe ar a sleper vnslyȝe, þat mon may slyde hider; / Now ar ȝe tan as-tyt! Bot true vus may schape, / I schal bynde yow in your bedde, þat be ȝe trayst" (lines 1209–11). In employing familiar courtly love metaphors of capture and bondage, she does nothing to alleviate Gawain's uneasiness. Their interchange is characterized throughout by tension as Gawain attempts to extricate himself from his vulnerable position while the lady capitalizes on his discomfort.

As the lady's first visit proceeds, her intention to seduce the hero becomes increasingly evident. Her major strategy is to appeal to his reputation:[9] "Sir Wowen ȝe are, / Þat alle þe worlde worchipez quere-so ȝe ride; / Your honour, your hendelayk is hendely praysed" (lines 1226–28). Taking advantage of the importance reputation plays in a knight's self-concept, she attempts to manipulate Gawain by insisting on her own definition of him. The perception of his excellence that she adopts is purely social and physical. After expressing pleasure in entertaining "hym þat al lykez" (line 1234), she offers him her "cors, / Yowre awen won to wale" (lines 1237–38). While her words could be innocently

---

9. Benson, *Art and Tradition in* Sir Gawain and the Green Knight, pp. 218–26.

intended,[10] Gawain's response indicates that he interprets them as a direct sexual proposal. He quickly denies that he is the man of whom she speaks, tactfully protesting that he is unworthy of such an honor as she proposes and offering to make himself worthy of her through word and deed.

Gawain's answer dramatizes how his own idea of knightly excellence differs from the one the hostess seems to espouse. He depicts the high-minded courtly image of woman as an unattainable ideal, inspiring knights to pursue perfection. In response the lady acknowledges Gawain's reputation for "prys" and "prowes" but expresses her interest in other charms (lines 1251–55):

> Bot hit ar ladyes innoȝe þat leuer wer nowþe
> Haf þe, hende, in hor holde, as I þe habbe here,
> To daly with derely your daynté wordez,
> Keuer hem comfort and colen her carez,
> Þen much of þe garysoun oþer golde þat þay hauen.

The lady willfully interprets Gawain's courtesy to consist in his accomplishment as courtly lover, a perception quite different from that implied in the pentangle. She attempts through banter to force him into conforming to a definition of knighthood wherein sensual imperatives supersede pentangle ideals. Conversely, Gawain attempts to reinstate his own more comprehensive and more moral definition of himself.

Although Gawain deflects the lady's advances, her strategy effectively engages his concern. When the lady challenges his identity, Gawain betrays his anxiety about correct knightly deportment "'Querfore?' quoþ þe freke, and freschly he askez, / Ferde lest he hade fayled in fourme of his castes" (lines 1294–95).

10. "My cors" could be a periphrasis for "me," and the line "ye ar welcum to my cors" construed as "your presence is very welcome to me"; see Burrow's discussion of the ambiguity of these lines. Burrow, *A Reading of Sir Gawain and the Green Knight*, pp. 81–82.

CONCEPTS OF CHIVALRY

Since knights depend on others to substantiate their reputations, the lady's challenge makes Gawain insecure. She tries to seduce Gawain into abandoning his personal values so as to merit her esteem. In view of the hero's knightly concern for public image as well as private ideals, her temptation is most appropriate.

Knowing the conventions of seduction, Bertilak's lady attempts to incorporate them into a definition of knightly manners (lines 1297–1301):

> "So god as Gawayn gaynly is halden,
> And cortaysye is closed so clene in hymseluen,
> Couth not lyȝtly haf lenged so long wyth a lady,
> Bot he had craued a cosse, bi his courtaysye,
> Bi sum towch of summe tryfle at sum talez ende."

Her description of Gawain neatly subverts the pentangle definition of chivalry. Where the pentangle asserted that the hero's "clannes and his cortaysye croked were neuer" (line 653), Bertilak's lady drops the "clannes" from Gawain's courtesy. An echo is there in the adverb *clene*, which funtions to isolate "cortaysye" as Gawain's distinctive characteristic. In the lady's perception a knight should attempt to kiss a beautiful woman; Gawain accepts a kiss because his idea of courtesy includes the negative injunction not to offend women. Thus the first morning's struggle ends in stalemate — neither participant succeeds in converting the other to his or her idea of chivalry.

After the ambiguous game of courtship and manners played out in Gawain's room, the poem returns to the host's outdoor activities. In the dividing of the quarry, Bertilak follows the ritual prescribed in manuals of the hunt. Barron addresses the purpose of these technical passages, arguing that medieval readers would note correspondences among the kill and division of the prey, the bedroom scenes, and medieval executions of traitors.[11] Although his case is historically documented, Barron's argument depends

11. Barron, *Trawþe and Treason*, pp. 30–75.

106

on the intrusion of modern sensibilities into the act of reading. The descriptions of slaughter are not calculated to disturb us deeply. Instead the poem asks readers to admire the action. The hunters are "lerned" (line 1170) in their craft. In butchering the quarry "derely . . . as þe dede askez" (line 1327), the best knights display the skills appropriate to their rank. The adverbs describing the hunters' actions express approval: "lystily" (line 1334), "lufly" (line 1606), "ful stoutly" (line 1364), and "aryȝt" (line 1911). The vocabulary describing the hunt expresses its aristocratic propriety, and it echoes the poem's praise of indoor displays of courtly manners. Nonetheless, the scenes of ritual slaughter remind readers of the inevitable human mortality that aristocratic games attempt to transcend.

After the exchange of winnings and a jovial agreement to renew the contract, the second day repeats the pattern of the first. Bertilak and his men follow a boar in an exhilarating chase, while Gawain lies in bed being pursued by the lady. Once again the host's unambiguous outdoor activities oppose his wife's highly charged pursuit of the hero. The hero's indoor occupation is as aristocratic as the hunt and is frequently described with comparable approval, but the precise conventions of the outdoor game contrast with the indeterminate rules followed indoors. While hunt manuals generally agree on the rules of the chase, fourteenth-century texts, from moralist tracts to romances, offer a perplexing abundance of conflicting guidelines for indoor behavior. Although the outdoor hunt is physically taxing, it seems less dangerous and stressful than Gawain's indoor pastimes.

Readers may wonder why the hero agrees to subject himself to a second opportunity for temptation, choosing to entertain the lady in his room rather than to hunt with the host or simply to bolt his bedroom door. On the first day he was caught unaware, but on the second morning he anticipates a visit from Bertilak's wife. While Gawain's compliance is essential to the plot, the lady's tactics on the second day suggest another explanation for his continued participation in the game of courtship. Gawain's choice of the lady's company derives from the theme of knightly identity in *Sir Gawain and the Green Knight*. On one level the hostess appeals to Gawain as a woman to a man, and his suppressed sexual desire draws him to her. But much more emphatically she addresses Gawain as a lady to a knight. The hero invites her company because he is driven by the need to prove himself the pentangle knight in her eyes.

The lady returns on the second morning to try to change Gawain's mind: "his mode for to remwe" (line 1475), and this time the hero welcomes her graciously. However, the hostess wonders whether her guest can be Gawain because he appears to have forgotten the conventions she expounded on the previous day. She renews the discussion of ideal chivalric deportment and the question of the visitor's identity, reminding him of her instructions on winning kisses: "'Quere-so countenaunce is coupe quikly to clayme; / Þat bicumes vche a knyȝt þat cortaysy vses'" (lines 1490–91). While Gawain diplomatically attributes his reticence to an unwillingness to be shamed by a refusal, the lady boldly asserts that Gawain cannot be refused, being strong enough "'to constrayne wyth strenkþe, ȝif yow lykez, / Ȝif any were so vilanous þat yow devaye wolde'" (lines 1496–97). The lady's suggestion that Gawain should rape anyone who is "vilanous" enough to refuse him comically dramatizes the distance between the sexual conception of courtliness that she adopts and Gawain's more spiritual chivalry. She subverts the pentangle idea of courtesy, which, fused with "clannes" and "pité," surely includes the moralist's injunction that knights do no harm to women.

A widely accepted intepretation of the temptation scenes is that they reflect uncourtly models. Burrow finds echoes of fabliaux,[12] and Benson detects the influence of medieval "Potiphar's Wife" tales.[13] Neither comparison satisfactorily accounts for the courtliness of both participants. Their behavior reflects

---

12. Burrow, *A Reading of* Sir Gawain and the Green Knight, pp. 74–77.
13. Benson, *Art and Tradition*, pp. 45–55.

different texts within the courtly tradition. Gawain's pentangle chivalry includes the religious idealism of knightly manuals such as Ramon Lull's *Le Libre del Orde de Cavalleria*. By contrast, the hostess takes her notion of chivalry from French romance. On the first day she casts Gawain as the character who never refuses an attractive woman.[14] On the second morning she adopts a loftier image of knighthood from the romances of *fin' amors* (lines 1512–19):

> "And of alle cheualry to chose, þe chef þyng alosed
> Is þe lel layk of luf, þe lettrure of armes;
> For to telle of þis teuelyng of þis trwe knyȝtez,
> Hit is þe tytelet token and tyxt of her werkkez,
> How ledes for her lele luf hor lyuez han auntered,
> Endured for her drury dulful stoundez,
> And after wenged with her walour and voyded her care,
> And broȝt blysse into boure with bountees hor awen."

Love is not only a game ("layk") to Bertilak's lady; it is also the learning ("lettrure") of arms. Discounting other chivalric texts, she defines the knight exclusively as lover. The lady describes a romance like Chrétien's *Le Chevalier de la Charette*, but, ironically, the knight she speaks of is not the Gawain of that tale. It is Launcelot who endures many pains for Guinevere's love and later avenges her and enjoys bliss in bower. Bertilak's wife offers Gawain a more refined and idealized image of sexuality than that of the previous morning, but one which remains unacceptable to the pentangle knight.

In answer, Gawain returns to "þe lettrure of armes," the literature of chivalry, asserting that her study of the subject differs from his own (lines 1540–45):

> Bot to take þe toruayle to myself to trwluf expoun,
> And towche þe temez of tyxt and talez of armez

14. Derek Brewer, "Courtesy and the *Gawain* Poet," in John Lawlor, ed., *Patterns of Love and Courtesy*, pp. 80–84.

> To yow þat, I wot wel, weldez more slyȝt
> Of þat art, bi þe half, or a hundreth of seche
> As I am, oþer euer schal, in erde þer I leue,
> Hit were a folé felefolde, my fre, by my trawþe.

While Gawain's assertion ostensibly compliments the lady for her erudition and neatly extricates him from the difficult position in which he is placed, it is something other than a courteous gesture of humility. The hero implies that for himself, and for knights like him, "a hundreth of seche," the study of "trwluf" in romance and tales of arms is irrelevant, "a folé felefold." Although the subject interests women like herself, it does not concern the pentangle knight.

Although each participant in the verbal exchange is highly accomplished, Gawain emerges successful according to the narrator's assessment of the second day's test, for the hero maintains the integrity of his ideals (lines 1549–53):

> Þus hym frayned þat fre, and fondet hym ofte,
> For to haf wonnen hym to woȝe, what-so scho þoȝt ellez;
> Bot he defended hym so fayr þat no faut semed,
> Ne non euel on nawþer halue, nawþer þay wysten
>   bot blysse.

The narrator seems to accept Gawain's spiritual definition of courtesy, wherein seduction would have been "to haf wonnen him to woȝe." At the same time he acknowledges the lady's point of view ("what-so scho þoȝt ellez"), suggesting that from her perspective there would be no harm in Gawain's giving in to her.[15] Finally, the narrator's position is indeterminate, for the second day ends with "non euel on nawþer halue."

The second evening follows a similar pattern to the first except that the lady flirts at dinner in a way that upsets Gawain,

---

15. Such would be the line's meaning for first-time readers; once the plot is known, the interjection would remind readers of the complicity of the lady, Bertilak, and Morgan la Faye.

although "he nolde not for his nurture nurne hir aȝaynez" (line 1661). While outwardly polite, Gawain experiences inner turmoil. He is "al forwondered. . ., and wroth wyth hymseluen" (line 1660). The tension in the situation lies in Gawain's conflicting obligations and impulses. His good breeding makes it unthinkable for him to repulse the lady directly, however much his religious convictions and his loyalty to his host might appear to be compromised by her advances. Moreover, Gawain's annoyance with himself suggests that he finds the lady's advances increasingly difficult to resist. Gawain asks to leave the next morning, perhaps as much to escape temptation as to assure his finding the Green Knight, but Bertilak insists that he stay, giving his oath ("trawþe") that Gawain will be at the Green Chapel in time. The host insists on a repetition of the previous two days, with Gawain lying in bed while he hunts and then an exchange of winnings in the evening. However, in this third instance, he adds a comment which implicates him in Gawain's test (lines 1679–82):

> For I haf fraysted þe twys, and faythful I fynde þe.
> Now "þrid tyme þrowe best" þenk on þe morne,
> Make we mery quyl we may and mynne vpon joye,
> For þe lur may mon lach when-so mon lykez.

Bertilak's words suggest that he knows more about Gawain's behavior than his daily absence warrants. Furthermore, the lines carry a powerful resonance of the memento mori *topos*, suggesting Gawain's upcoming encounter with the Green Knight and subtly linking the host with Gawain's opponent. This reminder of Gawain's impending fate prepares readers for the subtle shift in the nature of the third day's temptation.

Dressed more seductively than ever for the final onslaught, Bertilak's lady wakes Gawain from a deep sleep. He had been dreaming of his death: "How þat destiné schulde þat day dele hym his wyrde / At þe grene chapel" (lines 1752–53). In contrast to these grim thoughts of mortality, the lady appears as a shining emblem of life, an image delineated earlier in the comparison with her aged companion. Besides her obvious physical charms, her attraction now lies not only in her ability to validate Gawain's identity but also in the vital force she represents. On this day the hero comes closest to accepting her advances. In view of the approach of death the knight might be expected to follow Bertilak's advice and make merry while he can. The narrator powerfully conveys the effect the lady's presence has on Gawain as "Wiȝt wallande joye warmed his hert" (line 1762). Each of the alliterating words conveys a sense of vitality and of forces difficult to control.

The third temptation scene comes across ambiguously. From the aristocratic point of view it is a virtuoso performance of courtly manners: "...al watz blis and bonchef þat breke hem bitwene, and wynne. / Þay lanced wordes gode, / Much wele þen watz þerinne" (lines 1764–67). These lines characterize the interchange as joyous play. The metaphor of jousting illustrates the element of controlled ritual in the exchange between lady and knight. But subsequent lines offer a moralist perspective: "Gret perile bitwene hem stod, / Nif Maré of hir knyȝt mynne" (lines 1768–69). The comment has special significance for readers informed of the poem's ending, for, in view of the Green Knight's identity, the hero is imperiled by more than the stain of sin. His obligation to show courtesy to women strains his loyalty to the host as well as his religious fealty: "He cared for his cortaysye, lest craþayn he were, / And more for his meschef ȝif he schulde make synne, / And be traytor to þat tolke þat þat telde aȝt" (lines 1773–75). Nevertheless, he manages to hold together his pentangle ideals by deflecting the lady's offers gently, despite his own desire.

Although Gawain wins the battle to preserve his "clannes," the hostess finally succeeds in making him abandon his version of knighthood. At first the hero seems to have maintained his pentangle identity, for the lady adopts the pose of abandoned lover and gives up her seduction attempt. But in parting she persuades Gawain to accept a girdle which she claims will protect

the wearer. She makes him promise to conceal it from her lord —
an act which violates the oath made in the Exchange of Winnings
pact. In agreeing to "lelly layne" the girdle from Bertilak, Gawain
accepts the romance version of chivalry, in which loyalty to the
mistress supersedes bonds between knights. Like a lover he will
wear the lady's "drurye" on his quest.

Gawain's knightly ethos proves inadequate in sustaining him
against certain death. Tempted by the promise of life, the hero
succumbs, abandoning his high ideals for a more self-serving
compromise. After the dramatization of Gawain's dread of death
and of the seductiveness of life, the power of the final temptation
can be appreciated. The narrator gives a glimpse of Gawain's
inner thought as (lines 1855–58)

> hit come to his hert
> Hit were a juel for þe jopardé þat him iugged were:
> When he acheued to þe chapel his chek for to fech,
> Myȝt he haf slypped to be vnslayn, þe sleȝt were noble.

Having rejected a costly ring, Gawain perceives the superior
utility of the magic talisman and calls it a "juel." Then, with an
apparently unconscious verbal conjuring trick, he transforms his
dubious actions "slypped" and "sleȝt" into something honorable.
While Gawain's rationalization is perfectly understandable, the
text draws attention to its irony. Gawain's laudable struggle to
maintain his pentangle values gives way as he assures himself of
the nobility of his stratagem.

Gawain's lapse demonstrates a weakness in his idealistic chivalric ethos. When he must squarely confront a death devoid of
honor — the kind of end most of humanity experiences — his
knightly defiance fails him. Setting out on his journey, Gawain
places his trust in God, but he cannot maintain his faith in the
face of a more tangible alternative. Love of life and fear of death
are strong enough to make Gawain forget the complex demands
of his pentangle chivalry. Because she promises him an escape

from his fate, he at last accepts the lady's morality in place of his own.

Upon Gawain's acceptance of the girdle, a gulf opens up between his private and public selves, for his actions no longer conform to the identity defined in the pentangle. Alone in his room, the hero whose heraldic symbol signifies "trawþe" now acts with unchivalric cunning as he "Lays vp þe luf-lace þe lady hym raȝt, / Hid hit ful holdely, þer he hit eft fonde" (lines 1874–75). Gawain's descent from exemplary knightly behavior to lowborn craftiness is mirrored in the hunt taking place outside.[16] Bertilak's capture of a common fox—"þe schrewe" (line 1896), "þis wyly" (line 1905), "þis foule fox felle" (line 1944)—instead of the aristocratic beasts of the previous days reflects Gawain's knightly degeneration.

Gawain's subsequent confession, much debated by critics, seems to me to distinguish his violation of chivalric conduct from a sin in the Christian sense. The immediate juxtaposition of Gawain's hiding the girdle and his confession could be read as an indication of the soiled state of his soul as he undertakes the quest. He could be making an invalid confession.[17] But the poem fails to indicate that there is anything sinful in Gawain's intention to conceal the girdle from the host; instead there is the assurance that Gawain's confessor "asoyled hym surely and sette him so clene / As domezday schulde haf ben diȝt on þe morn" (lines 1883–84). Possibly Gawain's confession draws attention to his self-deception,[18] but by conventional Christian standards he has committed no grievous sin in taking the girdle.[19] He intends to cheat at a game of no great significance to save his life.[20]

16. Savage, *The Gawain Poet*, p. 5.

17. Burrow, *A Reading of* Sir Gawain and the Green Knight, pp. 104–10; Braswell, *The Medieval Sinner*, pp. 97–98; Jacobs, "Gawain's False Confession," pp. 433–35.

18. Engelhardt suggests that Gawain represses his fault, taking refuge "in superstition and a false conscience." Engelhardt, "The Predicament of Gawain," p. 222.

19. Stevens argues that it is a venial sin. Stevens, "Laughter and Game in *Sir Gawain and the Green Knight*," pp. 76–77. See also Thomas D. Hill, "Gawain's Jesting Lie: Toward an Interpretation of the Confessional Scene in *Sir Gawain and the Green Knight*," *SN* 52 (1980): 279–84.

20. Tolkien suggests that the confession is introduced to illustrate the difference between morals and gamesmanship. J. R. R. Tolkien, "*Sir Gawain and the Green Knight*," in *The Monsters and the Critics*, pp. 89–92.

Nonetheless, the violation of an agreement, whether made in jest or in earnest, represents a breach of knightly ethics. As the fourth fitt demonstrates, Gawain's violation of "trawþe" can be taken as a minor infraction, easily excusable under the circumstances; it can be transformed into a positive affirmation of life, or it can be condemned as an irredeemable departure from knightly ideals.

Chapter 8

Judgment and Meaning: Fitt 4

lthough the fourth fitt repeats some of the patterns of the second, with the hero arming himself, departing from the comfort of the court, and resuming his quest, it is an altered Gawain who sets out. The cold winter weather and the crowing of the cock function as reminders of human mortality, but the hero who formerly asserted his raw courage in the face of destiny—"What may mon do bot fonde?" (line 565)—now bears the girdle as a sign of his failure of nerve.

Attuned to heraldic imagery by the narrator's emphasis on the hero's shield, readers ought to pause and consider the implications of Gawain's altered coat of arms. A surcoat with the pentangle emblazoned on it reminds readers of the knight's aspirations: "His cote wyth þe conysaunce of þe clere werkez / Ennurned vpon veluet" (lines 2026–27). But over this heraldic device Gawain wears the green girdle: "ȝet laft he not þe lace, þe ladiez gifte, / Þat forgat not Gawayn for gode of hymseluen" (lines 2030–31). The narrator draws attention to the two contrasting colors: "Þe gordel of þe grene silke, þat gay wel bisemed, / Vpon þat ryol red cloþe þat ryche watz to schewe" (lines 2035–36). Interpretation depends on the values that readers attach to the contrasting symbols at this point. Barron points out some of their possibilities: "... an emblem of self-love jux-

117

taposed with one of *afyance* in God and *felaʒschyp* to fellow-man,"[1] a symbol of "*trawþe*" contrasted to one of "*untrawþe*."[2] While it certainly suggests these contrasts, the poem also insists on a particular interpretation of the girdle. Gawain does not wear it "for wele" (line 2037) or "for pryde of þe pendauntez" (line 2038), "Bot for to sauen hymself, when suffer hym byhoued, / To byde bale withoute dabate of bronde hym to were / oþer knyffe" (lines 2040–42). Innocent of avarice or vanity, Gawain wears the girdle solely for protection in his meeting with the Green Knight.

If the red of the surcoat symbolizes chivalric aspirations, the green of the girdle serves as a reminder of the human mortality — love of life and fear of death — which undermines Gawain's attempt to achieve perfection in his secular vocation of knighthood. As Barron points out, the vocabulary describing Gawain's motives is ambiguous ("sauen," "suffer," "bale").[3] Its Christian resonances remind readers of the moralist perspective on death. Gawain's altered emblem suggests that he confronts his mortality with neither pious faith in God nor knightly confidence in his prowess. The green bar which now crosses the pentangle signifies that its unity is broken.

Lest readers be tempted to judge Gawain too harshly, the guide serves as a foil to him,[4] just as the court does in the second fitt. Opposed to the hero who aspires nobly but whose idealism is sabotaged by his instinct for survival is the guide with his pragmatic approach to heroism: " 'For alle þe golde vpon grounde I nolde go wyth þe' " (line 2150). The guide tempts Gawain to take the safest way out of his dilemma by not visiting the chapel at all. Gawain does not succumb to this temptation but instead resolves

1. Barron, *Trawþe and Treason*, p. 108.
2. Barron cites Green, "Gawain's Shield and the Quest for Perfection," p. 192; and A. K. Hieatt, "*Gawain and the Green Knight*: Pentangle, *luf-lace*, numerical structure," in Alastair Fowler, ed. *Silent Poetry: Essays in Numerological Analysis*, p. 121.
3. Barron, *Trawþe and Treason*, p. 108.
4. Paul Delany, "The Role of the Guide in *Sir Gawain and the Green Knight*," *Neophil* 49 (1965): 250–55.

to trust in God. While readers may justifiably see irony in the brave assertions of a man protected by a magic talisman, Gawain seems sincere.[5] Once the guide leaves, Gawain's demeanor does not change. The green girdle does remarkably little to dispel his anxiety as he inspects the Green Chapel. As he prepares to accept the Green Knight's blow, Gawain seems to place little confidence in the baldric.[6]

By moralistic and heraldic standards Gawain's use of the lady's gift is blameworthy. His superstitious reliance on the girdle goes against Christian principles, while his use of a magic talisman violates contemporary laws of arms.[7] According to romance ethics, Gawain is not culpable for using magic against a supernatural foe. Invincible swords, protective rings, and other useful tokens are commonplace in romance.

Nonetheless, in his encounter with the Green Knight, Gawain behaves less like a romance hero than like an ordinary human being. The magic girdle does little to diminish Gawain's terror. The size of the opponent's ax "watz no lasse bi þat lace þat lemed ful bryȝt" (line 2226). Indeed, Gawain's pretended fearlessness as he bares his neck belies his true feelings. His reflexive shrinking from the first blow undercuts his heroic posing. In a departure from romance conventions the powers of the antagonist dwarf those of the hero. The Green Knight's taunting comparison of his own courage with Gawain's prompts the reflection that the game is grossly unfair: "...þaȝ my hede falle on þe stonez, / I con not hit restore" (lines 2282–83). In accepting the return blow, the hero seems at once comic and admirable. Gawain's fear brings him into the sphere of ordinary men, but his resolve distinguishes him.

5. Not all readers agree: Delany argues that Gawain's "show of virtue before the guide was at best self-deception and at worst pious hypocrisy." Ibid., p. 54.

6. Shedd, "Knight in Tarnished Armor," p. 9; Donald Howard, "Structure and Symmetry in *Sir Gawain*," *Speculum* 39 (1964): 429; Tolkien, "*Sir Gawain and the Green Knight*," p. 102.

7. Laila Gross, "Gawain's Acceptance of the Girdle," *An&Q* 12 (1973–74): 154–55; G. A. Lester, "Gawain's Fault in Terms of Contemporary Law of Arms," *N&Q* 221 (1976): 392–93.

CONCEPTS OF CHIVALRY

From the start of the poem the Green Knight functions as an opponent of chivalry, but once the test is over, the perspective that he reflects changes. After administering the three strokes, he watches Gawain leap up from his knees with his sword in hand, fearlessly ready to do battle, and "in hert it hym lykez" (line 2335). For the first time we see the challenger's inner thoughts. Surprisingly, his approval reflects a heraldic admiration of military aggression rather than a moralistic condemnation. The Green Knight's other identity as Bertilak, the jovial host, explains his approval of Gawain, for Hautdesert embraces a social and military conception of chivalry similar to Camelot's. Bertilak's judgment is far more sympathetic than the hero's own (lines 2362–68):

> "...and sothly me þynkkez
> On þe fautlest freke þat euer on fote ȝede;
> As perle bi þe quite pese is of prys more,
> So is Gawayn, in god fayth, bi oþer gay knyȝtez.
> Bot here yow lakked a lyttel, sir, and lewté yow wonted;
> Bot þat was for no wylyde werke, ne wowyng nauþer,
> Bot for ȝe lufed your lyf; þe lasse I yow blame."

Interestingly, Bertilak criticizes only Gawain's lack of loyalty in breaking their agreement to exchange the third day's winnings. The hero's display of courage at the chapel apparently acquits him of cowardice in the tester's eyes. Shedd argues that the Green Knight tempers his judgment with "a mercy whose springs lie completely outside the chivalric code of conduct.... He passes review on Gawain simply as one enlightened human being on another."[8] But it should be noted that Bertilak appraises the hero in terms of other knights. He also compares Gawain's slight failing to other possible crimes against chivalry—keeping the girdle for its material value, "þat was for no wylyde werke"[9] or

8. Shedd, "Knight in Tarnished Armor," p. 10.
9. In the notes for this line the editors of the Oxford edition offer this translation: "That was not for any excellent piece of workmanship." *Sir Gawain and the Green Knight*, ed. Tolkien and Gordon, rev. Davis, p. 128.

seducing the host's wife, "ne wowyng nauþer" (line 2367). As a life-loving nobleman, Bertilak excuses Gawain's lapse because love of life prompted it. It affirms aristocratic values to think of Gawain as a superlative figure: the most faultless, a pearl by white peas.

Ironically, Gawain takes up the moralist point of view that the now tolerant challenger abandons. The hero is deeply shamed by the revelation of his flaw. Cursing cowardice and covetousness, he flings the girdle at Bertilak. In giving in to his fear of death, he feels that he has compromised his ideals. He regrets how his fear of death caused him to abandon his chivalric ethos: "For care of þy knokke cowardyse me taȝt / To acorde me with couetyse, my kynde to forsake, / Þat is larges and lewté þat longez to knyȝtez" (lines 2379–81). Having fallen from his ideals, he redefines himself: "Now I am fawty and falce, and ferde haf ben euer / Of trecherye and vntrawþe" (lines 2382–83). Given the purity of his aspirations, Gawain's vehement self-denunciation is understandable.

The hero's deep remorse contrasts with his tester's tolerant good will. In the spirit of playfulness that has characterized him both as challenger and as host,[10] Bertilak laughingly absolves Gawain of any crimes against chivalry (lines 2390–94):

> "I halde hit hardily hole, þe harme þat I hade.
> Þou art confessed so clene, beknowen of þy mysses,
> And hatz þe penaunce apert of poynt of myn egge,
> I halde þe polysed of þat plyȝt, and pured as clene
> As þou hadez neuer forfeted syþen þou watz fyrst borne."

Gawain has made restitution of the girdle, acknowledged his faults, and performed his penance. His confession is complete.[11]

---

10. Many readers, particularly exegetical critics, have missed the poem's playful elements; at the opposite extreme, Bowers ("*Gawain and the Green Knight* as Entertainment") downplays the poem's moralistic voice, seeing the Green Knight essentially as a practical joker.

11. See Burrow, *A Reading of* Sir Gawain and the Green Knight, pp. 127–31.

In Bertilak's eyes the hero is restored to his former excellence, "polysed" and "pured" once more. He offers Gawain the girdle as a token of the chivalric adventure just completed, inviting him to return to the castle to celebrate the New Year.

Rejecting Bertilak's absolution, Gawain holds onto his sense of blame. The hero's behavior at this point is complex. Although he adopts moralist terms, his eschewal of forgiveness is un-Christian. His sense of his fault as irreparable reflects the heraldic point of view in which a breach of honor becomes a permanent stain. Gawain does not accept Bertilak's absolution because his pentangle ethos, unlike Christianity, asserts that man is perfectible on earth.

For the knight who defined himself publicly and privately by a symbol connoting perfection, nothing can heal the wound to his sense of identity. If we consider the elevated notion of chivalry embodied in the pentangle, we appreciate that, for the hero, to fail a little means to fail utterly. Indeed, the virtues are so closely interlocked that insufficiency in one involves insufficiency in others.[12] Gawain's cowardice and his breach of faith with Bertilak compromise his identity as a warrior. At the same time the hero's stature as a Christian knight declines. Although the pentangle declares confidence in the power of spiritual succor, when faced with a challenge which, unlike battle, offers no possibility of safety, Gawain abandons his trust in the five joys of Mary and accepts the girdle. His religious faith falters, and Mary's joys, all associated with the promise of redemption, offer him no consolation. Finally, Gawain compromises his renowned courtesy when, on learning of Lady Bertilak's part in the attempt to discredit him, he reflexively denounces women. Without acknowledging how it compromises chivalry, the hero adopts the moralistic point of view that the challenger has abandoned, echoing the anti-feminist sentiments often found in medieval sermons.[13]

12. Spearing, *The* Gawain-*Poet*, p. 209.
13. G. V. Smithers, "What *Sir Gawain and the Green Knight* Is About," *MÆ* 32 (1963): 177.

In taking up the unchivalric invective of sermon, Gawain transforms the "honoured ladyez" of the courtly tradition into the beguiling temptresses of the alternative medieval ideology. Where formerly the lady had represented a mirror of the hero's knightly excellence, she now reflects a tarnished image. Like the antifeminist moralists of his age, Gawain projects his own weakness onto women.[14] He attempts to save face by arguing that since great Old Testament heroes fell on account of women he thinks he might be excused.

There is fitting irony in the revelation that, while Bertilak's lady performs as her husband's agent, he in turn acts for Morgan La Faye. Gawain subjects himself to the tests at Hautdesert because of his need to authenticate his reputation. Having remained in his hostess's company to prove himself the pentangle knight, the hero discovers that he has been scrutinized more intensely than he has imagined, for his dealings with the lady were being judged by both the Green Knight and Morgan La Faye. Although he sought judgment, such publicity is more than Gawain can bear. Not surprisingly, he refuses Bertilak's invitation "to com to þyn aunt" (line 2467).

Morgan La Faye's role as the plot's instigator disturbs many modern readers.[15] Morgan's hatred of Guinevere is inadequate as a motive for the action. Her animosity toward the queen has nothing to do with the testing of the hero which occupies most of the poem. Nonetheless, in this romance that examines conceptions of chivalry, Morgan's primary intention is "to assay þe

14. See Ferrante, *Woman as Image in Medieval Literature*, pp. 17–35.
15. See James R. Hulbert, "*Syr Gawayn and the Grene Knyght*," *MP* 13 (1915): 454; George Lyman Kittredge, *A Study of* Gawain and the Green Knight, p. 136; Albert B. Friedman, "Morgan Le Fay in *Sir Gawain and the Green Knight*," *Speculum* 35 (1960): 260–74. Witness also the number of attempts, some rather farfetched, to explain her role; for example, Denver Ewing Baughan, "The Role of Morgan le Fay in *Sir Gawain and the Green Knight*," *ELH* 17 (1950): 241–51; J. Eadie, "Morgain La Feé and the Conclusion of *Sir Gawain and the Green Knight*," *Neophil* 52 (1968): 299–304; Douglas M. Moon, "The Role of Morgain la Fee in *Sir Gawain and the Green Knight*," *NM* 62 (1966): 31–57; Mother Angela Carson, O.S.U., "Morgain la Fee as the Principle of Unity in *Gawain and the Green Knight*," *MLQ* 23 (1962): 3–16.

surquidré, ȝif it soth were / Þat rennes of þe grete renoun of þe Rounde Table" (lines 2457–58). In view of woman's function as arbiter of chivalry in the romance genre, it is appropriate that a woman should conceive the plot.

Ultimately the hero adopts a new image of himself. He vows to wear the girdle as a token of his imperfection (lines 2433–38):

> "Bot in syngne of my surfet I schal se hit ofte,
> When I ride in renoun, remorde to myseluen
> Þe faut and þe fayntayse of þe flesche crabbed,
> How tender hit is to entyse teches of fylþe;
> And þus, quen pryde schal me pryk for prowes of armes,
> Þe loke to þis luf-lace schal leþe my hert."

Where initially he blamed abstract vices for his lapse, and next he denounced women, Gawain speaks ultimately of "myseluen." For the pentangle, sign of his perfection, he substitutes the token of his weakness. The girdle serves as a reminder of mortality, "þe flesche crabbed," which deflects his quest for glory. Though Gawain cannot reconcile his lapse with the high idealism of pentangle chivalry, he remains uncompromising. He adopts the language of ascetic Christianity, speaking of the corruptibility of the flesh and the necessity for humility. His final pose recalls that of knights like Henry of Lancaster and John Clanvowe who reject chivalry and adopt the voice of moralists.

For Gawain the girdle is a sign of personal failure. In place of the pentangle "bytoknyng of trawþe" (line 626), he wears "þe token of vntrawþe" (line 2509). The hero has abandoned his confidence in the possibility of his own perfection because of the revelation of his act of cowardice. His absolute idealism makes him unhappy with Bertilak's generous evaluation of him, and he sees himself as permanently disfigured by his slip: "For mon may hyden his harme, bot vnhap ne may hit, / For þer hit onez is tachched twynne wil hit neuer" (lines 2511–12). No longer fit to

wear the emblem of perfection, Gawain symbolically strips himself of his coat of arms, substituting the badge of his shame.[16]

Arthur's court refuses to accept Gawain's judgment of his
adventure. Not sharing the elevated idealism of the pentangle,
the lords and ladies had originally complained of the foolishness
of his assignation. When Gawain returns to the court wearing the
baldric, they rejoice at his physical safety: "And þus he commes
to þe court, knyȝt al in sounde. / Þer wakned wele in þat wone
when wyst þe grete / Þat gode Gawayn watz commen; gayn hit
hym þoȝt" (lines 2489–91). Appropriately, the court that embodies vitality highly values survival. They welcome him back as
"gode Gawayn," as if he were unchanged.[17] There is no suggestion that the laughter greeting Gawain's account of his dis-
grace comes from a sympathetic comprehension of his state of
mind. Instead it signifies relief in his physical survival.

As the court's conception of chivalry differs from Gawain's, so
does their conception of the green girdle. For them it conveys the
meaning that Bertilak's lady ascribes to it, a token of physical
invulnerability. As such the symbol validates their world view:
"For þat watz acorded þe renoun of þe Rounde Table, / And he
honoured þat hit hade euermore after" (lines 2519–20). For the
court the girdle symbolizes the triumph over mortality celebrated
in courtly games. Arthur's knights interpret Gawain's survival as
an affirmation of their belief in romance and heraldic ideologies.

Although the court's values are not as elevated as Gawain's,
their adoption of the girdle recalls a pentangle ideal that the hero
seems to have forgotten. Among the virtues represented in
Gawain's shield is "felaȝschyp," a concept which embraces both

16. A. Francis Soucy discusses Gawain's new heraldry at the end of the poem,
describing it as "a sign to the world of his sin and a reminder to himself of his
humanity." "Gawain's Fault: 'Angardez Pryde,'" *ChauR* 13 (1978): 175. While I agree
that Gawain presents the girdle as a badge of sin, he does not truly seem to accept
fellowship with the rest of humanity.

17. Burrow argues that here "Gawain is reassuming his everyday social identity" (*A
Reading of* Sir Gawain and the Green Knight, p. 157), an interpretation that does not
account for the difference between the hero's and the court's interpretation of the quest.

the sense of a chivalric community and the Christian concept of brotherly love. The court's gesture implies an acceptance of the hero's imperfection which Gawain himself lacks. By contrast to other, more tolerant perspectives in the poem, Gawain's absolutism seems un-Christian. The court's gesture reminds readers that the hero is not unique but one in a line of noble but flawed men from Aeneas down.[18]

Sir Gawain and the Green Knight ends with the various evaluations of the action unresolved. Bertilak, the court, and the hero have distinct perspectives, and there is no suggestion that they see outside their personal experience. A number of modern readers prefer to adopt a single point of view, some arguing that Gawain's disappointment is valid, others that the court has the saner perspective on life.[19] The arguments for both sides are appealing. Laughter and playfulness are balanced against Gawain's moral seriousness. While the romance elements in the poem insist on the importance of game in chivalric life, moralist passages stress the grave spiritual consequences of human action. Since the poem allows us into Gawain's consciousness, readers can be sympathetic to his point of view. On the other hand, his idealism limits his ability to make the relative judgments which the poem's ending seems to demand.

Finally, there are possible interpretations apart from those of characters in the romance. The revelation of the Green Knight's identity and of his household's complicity in the plot forces readers to review and to judge Gawain's behavior, just as Gawain himself does. In juxtaposing various views of the action, the poem allows readers to gain a personal understanding of the problems of knighthood. The salient features of the hero's portrait are his knightly idealism and his mortal vulnerability. These two realms of human experience are those which medieval moralists contrasted for didactic purposes and which medieval knights

18. See Alfred David, "Gawain and Aeneas," *ES* 49 (1968): 402–409.
19. See chap. 1 for a discussion of the opposing interpretations.

sometimes attempted to reconcile.[20] *Sir Gawain and the Green Knight* brings the two elements together in an original manner by dramatizing their conflict in the experience of an individual rather than in a static juxtaposition of images like the Wheel of the Ages of Man or "The Legend of the Three Living and the Three Dead." In this way the poem provokes readers into a meaningful evaluation of cultural commitments. The narrative challenges the ethos of chivalry by confronting its highest practitioner with his mortality. The hero errs because his pentangle idealism fails to account satisfactorily for human vulnerability. Although Gawain blames himself and the court congratulates him, the terms of the challenge prompt readers to see beyond either interpretation and to discern the tensions inherent in a form of chivalry that conforms to the fourteenth century's most idealistic definition of that institution.

Sir Gawain and the Green Knight dramatizes chivalry's limitations by showing that a militaristic emphasis on courage and defiance does not adequately prepare the knight for a passive, inglorious death. At the same time the poem is far more sympathetic than contemporary moralist attacks on knighthood. The hero's occupation as a fighter has not prepared him to accept without struggle the inevitability of death, but, paradoxically, because of his adherence to chivalric ideals, Gawain emerges as an exemplary figure, a "'perle bi þe quite pese'" (line 2364).

Including as it does an array of perspectives, *Sir Gawain and the Green Knight* permits a variety of interpretations. Unlike more obviously didactic works such as *Patience* and *Clannes*, *Sir Gawain and the Green Knight* does not begin with a thesis. Rather it creates a setting for the interplay of a number of theories. An argument can be made for the poem's didacticism, for the competing cultural myth of the moralists counters chivalry. However, the narrator does not explicitly replace the somewhat discredited expressions of chivalry with an exclusively Chris-

20. See chap. 4.

127

tian philosophy of life. Such an act of interpretation remains open to individual readers.

By adopting one of the perspectives inscribed in the poem and emphasizing certain elements over others, critics can make *Sir Gawain and the Green Knight* seem more definitively either an attack on or a celebration of the hero's chivalry. Nonetheless, the poem's competing narrative modes should serve to deny readers the comfortable position of unquestioningly accepting a fictional role. Since contrasting possibilities are given full play, *Sir Gawain and the Green Knight* draws attention both to man's potential for goodness and to his mortal weaknesses. The poem's competing narrative modes express the paradox of these two essential facets of human experience. Instead of adopting either a courtly or a moralist stance, readers can enjoy the poem's indeterminate structure and the finely balanced conclusion that makes *Sir Gawain and the Green Knight* continually available for reinterpretation.

Though modern readers may enjoy the text's unresolved ambiguity, the medieval response to its indeterminacy may have been different. Like modern critics, medieval readers might have been drawn to one of the ideological poles dramatized in the poem. Nonetheless, a more satisfactory solution to the challenge *Sir Gawain and the Green Knight* presents could have been to adopt a perspective broader than any offered in the poem itself. Observing the shortcomings in Gawain's self condemnation, as well as in the other characters' laughter, medieval readers might remember a judge of human action whose vision is more generous than the moralist's and more demanding than the court's. The poem ends with an invocation of Christ's grace: "Now þat bere þe croun of þorne, / He bryng vus to his blysse" (lines 2529–30). The problems delineated in the poem give vitality to these lines that might otherwise be dismissed as a conventional tag. Gawain has discovered his weakness and cannot forgive himself. Bertilak and the court forgive without fully understanding. This final prayer recalls that Christ has the generosity to offer mercy while fully comprehending human weakness.

Yet the text does not end with this appeal to the Christian theology of redemption. Inscribed at the end of the poem, in a somewhat later hand, according to Gollancz,[21] is the motto of the Order of the Garter: "Hony soyt qui mal pence." Somehow, this mysterious phrase, with its uncertain historical origin[22] and its tenuous connection to the poem,[23] seems a fitting capstone for *Sir Gawain and the Green Knight*. As a later addition to the manuscript it may be the response of a medieval reader. Yet, if so, its meaning is as unresolvable as the poem's.[24] In their heraldic context the words proudly defy anyone to think ill of the speaker's actions and imply that right will be asserted by military force, rather than moral argument. From this perspective the inscription would reject Gawain's delicacy of conscience and affirm Camelot's sense of fellowship. Conversely, the motto could be interpreted as an ironic moralist criticism of the unscrupulousness of contemporary knights. Mystifying as it is, this final reference to chivalry should serve as a warning to readers who search for a simple resolution of the problems delineated in *Sir Gawain and the Green Knight*. Instead of satisfying readers' questions, this final inscription sends us back to examine the text again. And finally, understanding the poem's conflicts is as important as arriving at an answer to the problems it defines.

21. Sir Israel Gollancz, Introduction, *Pearl, Cleanness, Patience, and Sir Gawain: Reproduced in Facsimile from the Unique MS. Cotton Nero A.x in the British Museum*, p. 8.

22. According to Juliet Vale, the motto probably refers to Edward III's claim to the French throne rather than to the apocryphal incident with the Countess of Salisbury's garter, Vale, *Edward III and Chivalry*, pp. 76–91.

23. H. L. Savage has tried, not very convincingly, to connect the poem to Enguerrand de Coucy, one of the Garter knights. Savage, *The Gawain-Poet*.

24. For three very different attempts to read the motto as a comment on the poem see Howard, *The Three Temptations*, pp. 251–52, who applies the message to Gawain; Moon, "The Role of Morgain la Fee in *Sir Gawain and the Green Knight*," p. 57, who takes it as a comment on Morgan la Faye; and Halpern, "The Last Temptation of Gawain," pp. 382–84, who takes it as a reference to the court.

PART THREE

Poems without Closure

Chapter 9

Conclusion

he tendency in Gawain criticism has been to suppress the final indeterminacy that I find fundamental to the experience of reading *Sir Gawain and the Green Knight*. Admittedly, accepting the poem's open-endedness means revising accepted notions of medieval poetry; thus my final chapter offers examples of other medieval texts to illustrate that it is not anachronistic to approach the poem by way of contemporary notions of textual indeterminacy and the role the reader plays in constructing meaning.

Indeterminate endings are not unusual in medieval poetry. Debate poems present opposed and frequently unresolved viewpoints. While the birds argue all day in Chaucer's *Parliament of Fowls*, their disagreements are never resolved. Instead the poem ends in a compromise that satisfies the dictates of both natural love and *fin' amours*. Similarly, Clanvowe's *Boke of Cupide* ends inconclusively. The argument begun by the nightingale and the cuckoo is postponed for continuation in another context, before the Queen's window at Woodstock, on Valentine's day. This device extends the debate outside the poem, perhaps to other literary forums, to the court, or, by implication, to the consideration of every reader of the poem. Other poems end by posing questions directly for readers; for example, Chaucer's Franklin creates an opening for discussion with the *demande* at the end of his tale. Finally, some poems have a circular movement in which heroes return to their point of departure with issues still unresolved. The dreamer in *Piers Plowman* must renew his spiritual quest, and in *Pearl* the dreamer remains engaged in the search for understanding.

The *Gawain* poet is not alone in recognizing the subjectivity and variety of audience response. Chaucer's *Troilus and Criseyde* is a case in point. At the end of the poem the narrator addresses a varied readership. For "yonge, fresshe folkes, he or she," presumably the readers who are seduced by the poem's depiction of carnal delights, the narrator offers a moralizing gloss, urging them to consider that "al nys but a faire / This worlde that passeth soone as floures faire" (5.1840–41). For "moral Gower" and "philosophical Strode" the narrator needs to provide no such explanation; rather he suggests that such wise readers may actually improve his text. Here he intimates that for the morally orthodox the poem may prove deficient. These two addresses posit diametrically opposed responses. Moreover, the narrator speaks to "every lady bright of hewe, / And every gentil womman, what she be" (5.1772–73). His plea that women not castigate him for Criseyde's guilt conjures up the image of a resisting feminine readership likely to object to the possible antifeminist bias in the portrayal of the heroine's inconstancy.[1] Like *Sir Gawain and the Green Knight*, *Troilus and Criseyde* dramatizes a number of possible responses to the problems raised in the text. Both poems suggest that the original audience had a greater tolerance for textual indeterminacy than modern scholars allow.

The special features of a manuscript culture may have fostered an understanding of the variety of potential response among medieval readers. For modern readers reading is usually a silent and private act, but evidence suggests that reading was often a

---

1. It might be said that here Chaucer anticipates contemporary theories which hold that the female reader experiences the text differently from a male. See Judith Fetterley, *The Resisting Reader*; Jonathan Culler, *On Deconstruction*.

shared activity in the Middle Ages.[2] In literature characters are frequently depicted sharing books — one thinks of Criseyde listening to the story of Thebes with her ladies when Pandarus visits her, of Jankin regaling the Wife of Bath with his misogynistic compendium, or of Dante's Paolo and Francesca reading a romance together.[3] In the famous *Troilus* frontispiece (Cambridge, Corpus Christi, MS 61, fol. 1v) the poet is depicted reading his work to a group of courtiers.[4] Although such a performance may never have actually taken place, it seems likely that in a manuscript culture secular writers would enjoy a more intimate relationship with readers than after the advent of print. Such a relationship might foster an awareness of the potential for multiple responses to a work.

My view of fourteenth-century culture posits an audience able to countenance multiple interpretative possibilities. It would be culturally chauvinistic to object that a medieval audience was incapable of such complex vision. To begin with, allegory demands that interpreters be fully conscious of multiple layers of meaning. Literal meaning may harmonize with the figural; for example, the parallels between Moses' deliverance of the Jews from Egypt and Christ's redemption of humanity make it easy to accept the former event as a prefiguration of the latter. In other instances the gulf between literal and allegorical interpretations may demand considerable effort by the reader. The disjunction between the scriptural letter and the exegetical interpretation of the Canticle of Canticles prompts Augustine to delight in the obscurity of interpretation: "Although we learn things which are said clearly and openly in other places, when these things are dug out of secret places, they are renewed in our comprehension, and being renewed, become more attractive."[5] For religious themes

2. See Ruth Crosby, "Oral Delivery in the Middle Ages," *Speculum* 11 (1936): 88–110.

3. For other examples see ibid., pp. 97–98.

4. For literary depictions of poets reading their works see ibid., pp. 94–96.

5. Augustine *Contra mendacium* 10.24. Quoted by Robertson, *A Preface to Chaucer*, pp. 55–56.

paradox and enigma lend a sense of sacred mystery. They present a challenge to which faith can rise. But the presence of paradox in secular texts leads to intellectual challenges of a different order.

In *Sir Gawain and the Green Knight* the clash between competing cultural values has the potential to call into question established ideologies. The poem treats the broad tension between courtly and Christian culture in a manner that draws readers into the dilemmas of knightly experience. A similar tension is at work in Chaucer's *Troilus and Criseyde*. The poem presents readers with unresolved contradictions. In exploring the conflict between courtly and moralist visions of the world, Chaucer's poem presents a powerful case for rejecting transient benefits for a more durable form of good, yet human love is perhaps never in all medieval literature so attractively presented.[6]

Even in Froissart's *Chroniques*, a work which lavishly celebrates fourteenth-century chivalry, we find cultural tensions expressed. Froissart generally writes in the heraldic mode. The Prologue to the *Chroniques* demonstrates a commitment to the ethic of military chivalry, proclaiming a heraldic interest in rendering a faithful account of military acts:

Afin que honorables emprises et nobles aventures et faits d'armes, lesquelles sont avenues par les guerres de France et d'Angleterre, soient notablement régistrées et mises en mémoire perpétuelle, par quoi les preux aient exemple d'eux encourager en bien faisant, je veux traiter et recorder histoire et matière de grand'louange.[7]

6. Muscatine sums up well the achievement of *Troilus*: "Two equally admirable, equally incomplete attitudes toward life are presented in the poem, and the value of each of these attitudes is communicated in the style specifically developed by tradition for its most effective realization. The negative element, the weakness inherent in each attitude, is presented through the reflection of the one on the other." Charles Muscatine, *Chaucer and the French Tradition*, p. 132. For a more detailed description of the poem's tensions see Paul Ruggiers, *The Art of* The Canterbury Tales, pp. 253–54.

7. Froissart, *Chroniques*, 1:1 ("So that the honorable undertakings and noble adventures and deeds of arms which occurred in the wars of France and England might be suitably registered and put in perpetual memory, so that the worthy might have an example to encourage them in doing well, I wish to record a history of great renown").

This initial statement lacks any moralistic reference to chivalry's part in the divine order. The major purpose for registering *faits d'armes* is that worthy knights (*les preux*) should have an example to encourage them, so that they will perpetuate chivalric activities. The major ideology of the *Chroniques* is represented from the outset as the celebration of the military aristocracy, the heraldic perspective.[8] Nonetheless, Froissart sometimes imports orthodox Christian morality in order to explain a breakdown in chivalric principles. After reporting the death of Richard II, Froissart offers some reflections on the variable nature of worldly fortunes:

> Or considérez seigneurs, rois ducs, comtes, prélats, et toutes gens de lignage et de puissance, comment les fortunes de ce monde sont merveilleuses et tournent diversement. Le roi Richard régna roi d'Angleterre vingt deux ans en grand' prospérité, tant que de tenir états et seigneuries; car il n'y eut oncques roi en Angleterre qui dépendît autant, à cent mil florins par an pour son hôtel seulement et son état tenir, que fit le roi Richard de Bordeaux.[9]

The notion of worldly instability is such a commonplace in the Middle Ages that readers expect a Boethian discussion of Richard's excessive attachment to the things of this world and of the necessity of turning from material to spiritual goods. Those expectations are violated by what follows:

8. Paul Archambault attributes Froissart's concern with surfaces and particulars to the influence of nominalism. Paul Archambault, *Seven French Chroniclers*, pp. 70–72. A simpler explanation lies in the heraldic mode of perception. Heraldic rolls celebrate the aristocracy through the delineation of particulars. Like rolls of arms and the Chandos Herald's *La vie du Prince Noir*, Froissart's *Chroniques* displays avid interest in deeds of arms, recording many of them.

9. Froissart, *Chroniques*, 3:368 ("Now consider lords, kings, dukes, counts, prelates, and all people of lineage and power, how the fortunes of this world are remarkable and shift variously. Richard reigned king of England for twenty two years in great prosperity, thus long holding estates and lordships; for there was never a king in England who spent as much by a hundred florins a year just for his household and to maintain his estate as did King Richard of Bordeaux").

Car moi, Jean Froissart, chanoine et trésorier de Chimay, le vis et con-
sidérai, et fus un quart d'an en son hôtel; et me fit très bon chère, . . . et
quand je me départis de lui ce fut à Windesore, à prendre congé, il me fit
par un sien chevalier . . . donner un gobelet d'argent dore d'or, pesant deux
marcs largement, et dedans cent nobles; dont je valus mieux depuis tout
mon vivant. Et suis moult tenu à prier de lui, et envis escripsis de sa
mort.[10]

Where one expects the observation of Fortune's instability to
elicit a universal Christian application, the narrative returns to
chivalric values. Instead of condemning Richard's material ex-
cesses, Froissart praises the sovereign's liberality and expresses his
personal loyalty. The invocation of Fortune's wheel leads to no
moral explanation; Richard's death is given no place in any
providential scheme.

Readers must assume the task of finding moral coherency in
the events Froissart has narrated, for neither chivalric nor moralist
explanations seem to suffice. Where many chroniclers place
events in an ideological framework, Froissart leaves his account of
Richard's death open-ended. There is an implicit political analysis in Froissart's account of Richard's unpopularity and his errors
in judgment. There is also a more medieval explanation in the
chronicler's reference to prophecy. A prediction made at Richard's
birth accurately forecasts his rise, while a passage from *The Brut*
anticipates the return of the crown to the House of Lancaster.[11]
The reader of the text must decide how much significance to allot
to each of the diverse ways of interpreting history.

Not all fourteenth-century texts challenge readers to entertain
multiple interpretative possibilities. When the demands of prop-
aganda usurp the requirements of art, literature attempts to

10. Ibid., 3:368–69 ("For I, Jean Froissart, canon and treasurer of Chimay, saw it
and reflected on it, and was in his household for a quarter of a year, and I lived very well
there, . . . and when I parted from him, it was at Windsor, to take leave he made me a
present through one of his knights . . . of a goblet of gilded silver weighing two marks,
with a hundred nobles inside, which increased my means my whole life. And I am
greatly bound to pray for him and am pained to write of his death").
11. Ibid., p. 369.

impose a narrow understanding on its audience. Much medieval poetry seeks to limit the reader's consideration of cultural conflicts. Even the texts that reflect cultural tension may not deliberately invoke the reader's judgment. While Froissart's *Chroniques* mirrors some of the contradictions inherent in fourteenth-century experience, the text does not necessarily challenge readers to confront them. By contrast *Sir Gawain and the Green Knight* engages its readers by posing problems rather than offering answers. It places cultural tensions in finely balanced opposition. In so doing, the poem does not ask readers to accept opposing values as equally valid — such relativism would be alien to medieval thought. Instead *Sir Gawain and the Green Knight* offers readers the opportunity to judge, allowing us to exercise free will by evaluating options for ourselves. Like other fourteenth-century masterpieces — *Pearl*, *Piers Plowman*, and some of Chaucer's works — *Sir Gawain and the Green Knight* addresses the tensions of late medieval life. Nevertheless its achievement is unique. No other poem captures as brilliantly the conflict between secular and courtly chivalry.

Bibliography

Primary Sources

Amis and Amiloun. Edited by MacEdward Leach. EETS, o.s., vol. 203. Oxford, 1937.

The Blickling Homilies of the Tenth Century. Edited by Rev. R. Morris. EETS, o.s., vol. 73. London, 1880.

Bouvet, Honoré. *The Tree of Battles of Honoré Bonet*. Translated by G. W. Coopland. Cambridge, Mass.: Harvard University Press, 1949.

Brandl, Alois, ed. *The Pride of Life: Quellen des Weltlichen Dramas in England vor Shakespeare*. Quellen und Forschungen zur Sprach und Culturgeschichte, 80 heft. Strassburg: Karl J. Trübner, 1898.

Chandos Herald. *La vie du Prince Noir*. Edited by Diana B. Tyson. Biehefte zur Zeitschrift fur Romanische Philologie, vol. 147. Tübingen: Max Niemeyer, 1975.

Chaucer, Geoffrey. *The Works of Geoffrey Chaucer*. Edited by F. N. Robinson. Boston: Houghton Mifflin, 1933; 2d ed., 1957.

Chrétien de Troyes. *Arthurian Romances*. Translated by W. W. Comfort. London and New York, 1914.

———. *Le Chevalier au Lion (Yvain)*. Edited by Mario Roques. Classiques Français du Moyen Âge, vol. 89. Paris: Champion, 1965.

———. *Le Chevalier de la Charette*. Edited by Mario Roques. Classiques Français du Moyen Âge, vol. 86. Paris: Champion, 1965.

———. *Cliges*. Edited by Alexandre Micha. Classiques Français du Moyen Âge, vol. 84. Paris: Champion, 1957.

———. *Erec et Enide*. Edited by Mario Roques. Classiques Français du Moyen Âge, vol. 80. Paris: Champion, 1963.

Clanvowe, John. *The Boke of Cupide*. Edited by V. J. Scattergood. In *The Works of Sir John Clanvowe*. Totowa, N.J.: Rowman and Littlefield, 1975.

———. *The Two Ways*. Edited by V. J. Scattergood. In *The Works of Sir John Clanvowe*. Totowa, N.J.: Rowman and Littlefield, 1975.

Death and Liffe. Edited by Israel Gollancz. In *Select Early English Poems*. London, 1930.

Froissart, Jean. *Les chroniques de Sire Jean Froissart*. Edited by J. A. C. Buchon. Paris: Société du Pantheon Litteraire, 1840.

Geoffrey of Monmouth. *Historia Regum Britanniae*. Edited by Acton Griscom. New York: Longmans, Green, 1929.

Geoffroi de Charny. *Le livre de chevalerie*. Edited by Kervyn de Lettenhove. In *Oeuvres de Froissart*, I:463-533.

———. "Le livre Messire Geoffroi de Charny." Edited by Arthur Piaget. *Romania* 26 (1987): 394-411.

Guillaume de Lorris et Jean de Meun. *Le Roman de la Rose*. Paris: Felix Lecoy, 1965-70.

Havelock the Dane. Edited by W. W. Skeat. EETS, extra series, vol. 4. London, 1868.

Henry of Lancaster. *Le livre de seyntz medicines*. Edited by E. J. Arnould. Anglo-Norman Text Society, no. 2. Oxford: Blackwell, 1940.

King Horn. Edited by J. Hall. Oxford, 1901.

Knight of Tour-Landry. *The Book of the Knight of la Tour-Landry*. Edited by Thomas Wright. EETS, o.s., vol. 33. London, 1906.

Lull, Ramon. *The Book of the Ordre of Chyualry*. Translated by William Caxton. EETS, o.s., vol. 168. London, 1926.

Mirk, John. *Mirk's Festial*. Edited by Theodor Erbe. EETS, extra series, vol. 96. London, 1905.

Nichols, John, ed. *A Collection of All the Wills of the Kings and Queens of England*. London, 1780.

Phillipe de Mézières. *Letter to King Richard II*. Translated by G. W. Coopland. New York: Barnes and Noble, 1976.

La queste del Saint Graal. Edited by Albert Pauphilet. Paris: Mario Roques, 1949.

The Siege of Caerlaverock. Edited by Gerald J. Brault. In *Eight Thirteenth Century Rolls of Arms in Anglo-Norman Blazon*. University Park: Pennsylvania State University Press, 1973.

Sir Gawain and the Green Knight. Edited by J. R. R. Tolkien and E. V. Gordon; 2d ed., revised by Norman Davis. Oxford: Clarendon Press, 1967.

Sir Gawain and the Green Knight. Edited by Theodore Silverstein. Chicago: University of Chicago Press, 1984.

Secondary Sources

Ackerman, Robert W. "Gawain's Shield: Penitential Doctrine in *Sir Gawain and the Green Knight*." *Anglia* 76 (1958): 254-65.

Archambault, Paul. *Seven French Chroniclers, Witnesses to History*. Syracuse, N.Y.: Syracuse University Press, 1974.

Auerbach, Erich. *Mimesis: The Representation of Reality in Western Literature*. Translated by W. A. Trask. Princeton, N.J.: Princeton University Press, 1953.

Baker, Audrey. "The Interpretation and Iconography of the Longthorpe Paintings." *Archaeologia* 96 (1955): 35-56.

BIBLIOGRAPHY

Barnie, John. *War in Medieval Society*. Ithaca, N.Y.: Cornell University Press, 1974.

Barron, W. R. J. *Trawpe and Treason*. Manchester: Manchester University Press, 1980.

Baughan, Denver Ewing. "The Role of Morgan Le Fay in *Sir Gawain and the Green Knight*." *ELH* 17 (1950): 241–51.

Bennett, Michael J. *Community, Class and Careerism: Cheshire and Lancashire Society in the Age of Sir Gawain and the Green Knight*. Cambridge Studies in Medieval Life and Thought. Cambridge: Cambridge University Press, 1983.

Benson, Larry. *Art and Tradition in* Sir Gawain and the Green Knight. New Brunswick, N.J.: Rutgers University Press, 1965.

——. *Malory's* Morte Darthur. Cambridge, Mass.: Harvard University Press, 1976.

Bloomfield, Morton W. "Episodic Motivation and Marvels in Epic and Romance." In *Essays and Explorations*. Cambridge, Mass.: Harvard University Press, 1970.

——. "*Sir Gawain and the Green Knight*: An Appraisal." *PMLA* 76 (1961): 7–19.

Bowers, R. H. "*Gawain and the Green Knight* as Entertainment." *MLQ* 24 (1963): 333–41.

Brandt, William J. *The Shape of Medieval History*. New Haven, Conn.: Yale University Press, 1966.

Braswell, Mary Flowers. *The Medieval Sinner*. East Brunswick, N.J.: Associated University Presses, 1983.

Brewer, Derek. "The Arming of the Warrior in European Literature and Chaucer." In Edward Vasta and Zacharias P. Thundy, eds. *Chaucerian Problems and Perspectives*. Notre Dame, Ind.: University of Notre Dame Press, 1979.

——. "Courtesy and the *Gawain* Poet." In John Lawlor, ed. *Patterns of Love and Courtesy*. Evanston, Ill.: Northwestern University Press, 1966.

——. "The *Gawain* Poet: A General Appreciation of Four Poems." *EIC* 7 (1967): 130–42.

Broes, Arthur T. "*Sir Gawain and the Green Knight*: Romance as Comedy." *Xavier University Studies* 4 (1965): 35–54.

Brown, Peter. *The Cult of the Saints*. Chicago: University of Chicago Press, 1981.

Burrow, J. A. *A Reading of* Sir Gawain and the Green Knight. New York: Barnes and Noble, 1966.

Butturf, Douglas R. "Laughter and Discovered Aggression in *Sir Gawain and the Green Knight*." *L&P* 22 (1972): 139–49.

Carson, Mother Angela, O.S.U. "Morgain la Fée as the Principle of Unity in *Gawain and the Green Knight*." *MLQ* 23 (1962): 3–16.

Chambers, E. K. *The Medieval Stage*. Oxford: Oxford University Press, 1925.

Christmas, Peter. "A Reading of Sir Gawain and the Green Knight." *Neophil* 58 (1974): 238–47.

Cohen, Kathleen. *Metamorphosis of a Death Symbol*. California Studies in the History of Art. Berkeley: University of California Press, 1973.

Cook, Robert G. "The Play Element in *Sir Gawain and the Green Knight*." *TSE* 13 (1963): 5–31.

Crosby, Ruth. "Oral Delivery in the Middle Ages." *Speculum* 11 (1936): 88–110.

Culler, Jonathan. *On Deconstruction*. Ithaca, N.Y.: Cornell University Press, 1982.

David, Alfred. "Gawain and Aeneas." *ES* 49 (1968): 402–409.

143

CONCEPTS OF CHIVALRY

Delany, Paul. "The Role of the Guide in *Sir Gawain and the Green Knight*." *Neophil* 49 (1965): 250–55.

Denholm-Young, N. *History and Heraldry: 1285 to 1310*. Oxford: Oxford University Press, 1965.

Eadie, J. "Morgain La Fee and the Conclusion of *Sir Gawain and the Green Knight*." *Neophil* 52 (1968): 299–304.

Emerson, Oliver Farrar. "Notes on *Sir Gawain and the Green Knight*." *JEGP* 21 (1922): 363–410.

Engelhardt, George J. "The Predicament of Gawain." *MLQ* 16 (1955): 218–25.

Everett, Dorothy. *Essays on Middle English Literature*. Oxford: Clarendon Press, 1955.

Ferguson, Arthur B. *The Indian Summer of English Chivalry*. Durham, N.C.: Duke University Press, 1960.

Ferrante, Joan. *Woman as Image in Medieval Literature*. New York: Columbia University Press, 1975.

Fetterley, Judith. *The Resisting Reader*. Bloomington: Indiana University Press, 1978.

Field, P. J. C. "A Rereading of *Sir Gawain and the Green Knight*." *SP* 68 (1971): 255–69.

Fish, Stanley. "Literature in the Reader: Affective Stylistics." *NLH* 2 (1970): 123–62.

Friedman, Albert B. "Morgan le Fay in *Sir Gawain and the Green Knight*." *Speculum* 35 (1960): 260–74.

Gallant, Gerald. "The Three Beasts: Symbols of Temptation in *Sir Gawain and the Green Knight*." *AnM* 11 (1970): 35–50.

Ganim, John M. "Disorientation, Style, and Consciousness in *Sir Gawain and the Green Knight*." *PMLA* 91 (1976): 376–84.

Goldhurst, William. "The Green and the Gold: The Major Theme of *Gawain and the Green Knight*." *CE* 20 (1958): 61–65.

Gollancz, Sir Israel. Introduction. *Pearl, Cleanness, Patience, and Sir Gawain: Reproduced in Facsimile from the Unique MS. Cotton Nero A.x in the British Museum*. EETS, o.s., vol. 162. London, 1923.

Green, Richard Firth. *Poets and Princepleasers*. Toronto: University of Toronto Press, 1980.

Green, Richard Hamilton. "Gawain's Shield and the Quest for Perfection." *ELH* 29 (1962): 121–39.

Gross, Laila. "Gawain's Acceptance of the Girdle." *AN&Q* 12 (1974): 154–55.

Haines, Victor Yelverton. *The Fortunate Fall of Sir Gawain*. Washington, D.C.: University Press of America, 1982.

Halpern, R. A. "The Last Temptation of Sir Gawain: Hony Soit Qui Mal Pence." *ABR* 23 (1972): 353–84.

Harvey, John. *The Black Prince and His Age*. Totowa, N.J.: Rowman and Littlefield, 1976.

Hieatt, A. K. "*Gawain and the Green Knight*: Pentangle, *luf-lace*, numerical structure." In Alastair Fowler, ed. *Silent Poetry: Essays in Numerological Analysis*. London, 1970.

Hill, Thomas D. "Gawain's Jesting Lie: Toward an Interpretation of the Confessional Scene in *Sir Gawain and the Green Knight*." *SN* 52 (1980): 279–84.

BIBLIOGRAPHY

Howard, Donald R. "Structure and Symmetry in *Sir Gawain.*" *Speculum* 39 (1964): 425–33.

———. *The Three Temptations: Medieval Man in Search of the World.* Princeton, N.J.: Princeton University Press, 1966.

Huizinga, J. *Homo Ludens.* London: Routledge & Kegan Paul, 1949.

———. *The Waning of the Middle Ages.* London: Arnould, 1924.

Hulbert, James R. "*Syr Gawayn and the Grene Knyȝt.*" *MP* 13 (1915): 433–62.

Hunt, Tony. "Gawain's Fault and the Moral Perspectives of *Sir Gawain and the Green Knight.*" *Trivium* 10 (1975): 1–18.

Hurtig, Judith. *The Armored Gisant Before 1400.* New York: Garland, 1979.

Iser, Wolfgang. *The Act of Reading.* Baltimore, Md.: Johns Hopkins University Press, 1978.

Jacobs, Nicolas. "Gawain's False Confession." *ES* 51 (1970): 433–35.

Jauss, Hans Robert. *Toward an Aesthetic of Reception.* Translated by Timothy Bahti. Theory and History of Literature, vol. 2. Minneapolis: University of Minnesota Press, 1982.

Johnson, Lynn Staley. *The Voice of the* Gawain-*Poet.* Madison: The University of Wisconsin Press, 1984.

Jones, Evan. *Medieval Heraldry.* Cardiff, 1943.

Keen, Maurice. *Chivalry.* New Haven, Conn.: Yale University Press, 1984.

Kilgour, Raymond L. *The Decline of Chivalry.* Cambridge, Mass.: Harvard University Press, 1937.

Kiteley, J. F. "The *De Arte Honeste Amandi* of Andreas Capellanus and the Concept of Courtesy in *Sir Gawain and the Green Knight.*" *Anglia* 97 (1961): 7–16.

Kittredge, George Lyman. *A Study of* Gawain and the Green Knight. Cambridge, Mass.: Harvard University Press, 1916.

Krappe, A. H. "Who *Was* the Green Knight." *Speculum* 13 (1938): 206–15.

Lester, G. A. "Gawain's Fault in Terms of Contemporary Law of Arms." *AN&Q* 221 (1976): 392–93.

Lewis, C. S. *The Allegory of Love.* Oxford: Clarendon Press, 1936.

McFarlane, K. B. *Lancastrian Kings and Lollard Knights.* Oxford: Clarendon Press, 1972.

Mathew, Gervase. *The Court of Richard II.* New York: W. W. Norton, 1968.

———. "Ideals of Knighthood in Late Fourteenth Century England." In *Studies in Medieval History Presented to F. M. Powicke.* Oxford: Oxford University Press, 1948.

Mehl, Dieter. *The Middle English Romance of the Thirteenth and Fourteenth Centuries.* London: Routledge and Kegan Paul, 1967.

Moon, Douglas M. "The Role of Morgain la Fee in *Sir Gawain and the Green Knight.*" *NM* 62 (1966): 31–57.

Moorman, Charles. *A Knyght There Was.* Lexington: University of Kentucky Press, 1967.

Muscatine, Charles. *Chaucer and the French Tradition.* Berkeley: University of California Press, 1957.

———. *Poetry and Crisis in the Age of Chaucer.* Notre Dame, Ind.: University of Notre Dame Press, 1972.

CONCEPTS OF CHIVALRY

Neaman, Judith S. "Sir Gawain's Covenant: Troth and *Timor Mortis.*" *PQ* 55 (1976): 30–42.

Ong, Walter J. "The Writer's Audience Is Always a Fiction." *PMLA* 90 (1975): 9–21.

Owst, G. R. *Literature and Pulpit in Medieval England.* Cambridge: At the University Press, 1933; rev. ed., Oxford: Oxford University Press, 1961.

Painter, Sidney. *French Chivalry.* Baltimore, Md.: Johns Hopkins Press, 1940.

Panofsky, Erwin. *Tomb Sculpture.* Edited by H. W. Janson. New York: H. N. Abrams, 1964.

Pearsall, Derek. "The Alliterative Revival: Origins and Social Backgrounds." In David Lawton, ed. *Middle English Alliterative Poetry and Its Literary Background.* Woodbridge, Suffolk: Boydell & Brewer, 1982.

Pearsall, Derek, and Elizabeth Salter. *Landscapes and Seasons of the Medieval World.* London: Elek Books, 1973.

Pierle, Robert C. *"Sir Gawain and the Green Knight*: A Study in Moral Complexity." *SQ* 6 (1968): 203–11.

Powicke, Michael. *Military Obligation in Medieval England.* Oxford: Clarendon Press, 1962.

Robertson, D. W. *A Preface to Chaucer.* Princeton, N.J.: Princeton University Press, 1962.

Ruggiers, Paul. *The Art of* The Canterbury Tales. Madison: University of Wisconsin Press, 1965.

Salter, Elizabeth. "The Alliterative Revival." *MP* 64 (1966): 146–50, 233–37.

———. *Fourteenth Century Poetry.* Oxford: Clarendon Press, 1983.

Sandler, Lucy Freeman. *The Psalter of Robert de Lisle.* London: Oxford University Press, 1983.

Savage, H. L. *The* Gawain-*Poet: Studies in His Personality and Background.* Chapel Hill: North Carolina University Press, 1956.

———. "A Note on Gawain and the Green Knight (700–2)." *MLN* 46 (1931): 455–57.

———. "The Significance of the Hunting Scenes in *Sir Gawain and the Green Knight.*" *JEGP* 27 (1928): 1–15.

Scattergood, V. J. "Literary Culture at the Court of Richard II." In V. J. Scattergood and J. W. Sherbourne, eds. *English Court Culture in the Later Middle Ages.* New York: St. Martin's Press, 1983.

Schnyder, Hans. "Aspects of Kingship in 'Sir Gawain and the Green Knight.'" *ES* 40 (1959): 289–94.

Scott-Giles, C. Wilfred. *The Romance of Chivalry.* London: J. M. Dent, 1929.

Shedd, Gordon M. "Knight in Tarnished Armor: The Meaning of *Sir Gawain and the Green Knight.*" *MLR* 62 (1967): 3–13.

Silverstein, Theodore. "The Art of Sir Gawain and the Green Knight." *UTQ* 33 (1964): 258–78.

Smithers, G. V. "What *Sir Gawain and the Green Knight* Is About." *MÆ* 32 (1963): 171–89.

Soucy, A. Francis. "Gawain's Fault: 'Angardez Pryde.'" *ChauR* 13 (1978): 166–76.

Spearing, A. C. *The* Gawain *Poet.* Cambridge: Cambridge University Press, 1970.

Speirs, John. *Medieval English Poetry: The Non-Chaucerian Tradition.* London: Faber and Faber, 1957.

146

BIBLIOGRAPHY

Stevens, Martin. "Laughter and Game in *Sir Gawain and the Green Knight.*" *Speculum* 47 (1972): 65–78.

Thiebaux, Marcelle. *The Stag of Love.* Ithaca, N.Y.: Cornell University Press, 1974.

Tolkien, J. R. R. "*Sir Gawain and the Green Knight.*" In *The Monsters and the Critics.* Boston: Houghton Mifflin, 1984.

Trask, Richard M. "Sir Gawain's Unhappy Fault." *SSF* 16 (1979): 1–9.

Tristram, Phillipa. *Figures of Life and Death in Medieval English Literature.* New York: New York University Press, 1976.

Vale, Juliet. *Edward III and Chivalry.* Suffolk: Boydell Press, 1982.

Vale, Malcolm. *War and Chivalry.* Athens: University of Georgia Press, 1981.

Whiting, B. J. "Gawain: His Reputation, His Courtesy, and His Appearance in Chaucer's *Squire's Tale.*" *MS* 9 (1947): 189–234.

Wright, N. A. R. "The *Tree of Battles* of Honoré Bouvet and the Laws of War." In C. T. Allmand, ed. *War, Literature, and Politics in the Late Middle Ages.*" New York: Barnes and Noble, 1976.

Index

149

INDEX

151